LIFE ON THE FUNNY FARM

Ann Cato

©2005 Dianne Taylor
All Rights Reserved

To the two and four legged stars of the book.
Thank you for enriching my life.

Contents

Chapter 1 - All Change..1

Chapter 2 - To Be or Not to Be?..8

Chapter 3 - The End of a Quest...12

Chapter 4 - The In-Laws...15

Chapter 5 - Making Ends Meet...18

Chapter 6 - The Villagers..21

Chapter 7 - Feathered Friends..24

Chapter 8 - Spring Brings a New Life..28

Chapter 9 - The Art of Kiddology..31

Chapter 10 - Peggy Joins the Team..35

Chapter 11 - A Champion is Born..39

Chapter 12 - Pork is on the Menu..42

Chapter 13 - Bringing Home the Bacon...45

Chapter 14 - Basil the Billy Goat..47

Chapter 15 - Porcine Pranks...50

Chapter 16 - Gertie Gets Annoyed..53

Chapter 17 - A Difficult Birth..55

Chapter 18 - Building Plans...57

Chapter 19 - The Plans are Put into Action.............................59

Chapter 20 - New Foundations...62

Chapter 21 - Farewell to Susie...65

Chapter 22 - Chantey to the Rescue...69

Chapter 23 - Trying the Gypsy Lifestyle...................................71

Chapter 24 - Home Produced Meat..75

Chapter 25 - Luck Runs Out..77

Chapter 26 - Surprise Announcement.......................................80

Chapter 27 - One Woman and a Dog.......................................83

Chapter 28 - The Dog Hotel Opens..85

Chapter 29 - Bill and Minnie...87

Chapter 30 - Doris Bows Out..89

Chapter 31 - Anthony and Cleopatra..91

Chapter 32 - Lot 39..94

Chapter 33 - The Auction..98

Chapter 34 - The Royal Show..101

Chapter 35 - Intruders..103

Chapter 36 - Free Range Turkeys...106

Chapter 37 - The Smiling Somali..108

Chapter 38 - Sale Day..111

Chapter 39 - Tess Comes Home...114

Chapter 40 - The Man from Italy..116

Chapter 41 - Christmas Shopping...119

Chapter 42 - Brer Fox Does his Worst...121

Chapter 43 - Sonasag Arrives...123

Chapter 44 - A Calf is Born...126

Chapter 45 - Turkey Trot...129

Chapter 46 - The First Family Holiday..131

Chapter 47 - A Somali Take-Over..135

Chapter 48 - Bovine Blunders..139

Chapter 49 - The Farm Gets a Makeover...................................141

Chapter 50 - Highland Fling...143

Chapter 51 - A Surprise Christmas Present...............................145

Chapter 52 – Biting off More than You Can Chew..........................148

Chapter 53 – Duped at an Auction..151

Chapter 54 – Graham is Put Through His Paces............................153

Chapter 55 – A Load of Bull...156

Chapter 56 – Waifs and Strays...158

Chapter 57 – Raffles..161

Chapter 58 – Ducking and Diving..164

Chapter 59 – Sex in the Country..166

Chapter 60 – Dicing with Danger..168

Chapter 61 – Staying Put...170

Chapter 62 – A Night Vigil...172

Chapter 63 – Angie's Undoing...175

Chapter 64 – Resurrection..177

Chapter 65 – Tail Ends...180

Chapter 66 – Puppies and Partying..182

Chapter 1
All Change

I stood still, rooted to the spot with nerves. My loving father was at my side. In a voice, которой didn't seem to belong to me, I whispered, "I think I need to go to the toilet." Rather testily my father replied, "It's too late now, you will have to wait until it's all over." No sooner had he spoken than the first strident notes of The Trumpet Voluntary rang out from the organ. I began to walk down the aisle of my small village church. A short while later I retraced my steps, no longer a 'spinster of this parish' but a married woman.

I met the man who was to become my husband three years earlier. I had moved to the City of Birmingham to study at a Teacher Training College and when I qualified, I found a position at a city school. After eighteen months of renting accommodation, I purchased a maisonette in one of the suburbs. Many of the neighbours were teachers so we had a great deal in common, and this led to a shared social life. One neighbour stood out from the others. Unlike us, he was not a teacher but a businessman. I would not describe him as handsome but his appearance was certainly striking. He was of medium height and built but he had a shock of bright ginger hair and a bushy red beard, which framed his face, conjuring up the image of a seafaring pirate. To accompany his unforgettable appearance, he had a personality to match- he managed to make his presence felt wherever he was. He was an out and out extrovert, always ready to take centre stage. He was the life and soul of any group he socialised with. Over the months we exchanged neighbourly pleasantries, but it was some months before Graham plucked up courage to pay me a visit.

The day Graham eventually asked me out on a date is one I remember clearly but for a very different reason. I cannot remember any time in my life without having a pet of some description. That morning a friend had taken me to a local veterinary surgery to pick up a kitten, which had been abandoned. I named the ginger and white kitten Charlie. He had a trusting, gentle nature. I was still busy settling Charlie into his new home when my doorbell rang. I opened the door to find Graham standing there. "Hello, I was wondering if you would like to go out this evening for a meal." His question hung in the air as I hurriedly asked him to come in.

I explained, "I must keep the door closed as I have just brought a new kitten home." Graham walked in and showed a diplomatic interest in the kitten but his question remained unanswered. Reluctantly I said, "It's kind of you to invite me out for a meal and any other time the answer would have been yes, but I can't leave Charlie alone in a strange home."

That was Graham's first insight into my passion for animals. When he complained bitterly that I thought more of the animals than of him, I would remind him of the passed up date, at least it was more original than washing my hair! I remember that day fondly as the one when two ginger Toms walked into my life! Graham was undeterred by my brush-off, he visited Charlie and regularly, bringing gifts of Salmon, Tuna and Pilchards. Charlie devoured his presents with relish, whilst I bore no jealousy at the absence of flowers or chocolates. The way to this woman's heart was definitely through her cat!

During our courtship I learnt that Graham had two passions in life, his work and golf. He ran his own transport firm with other members of his family; he worked long hours to make a success of the firm. I too, was committed to my work. I had gained rapid promotion and was Head of Department in an inner city secondary school. I was ambitious and planned to reach even greater heights in my career. Both of us knew where we wanted to go, and we hoped we would make a winning team.

We still remember our wedding day fondly. It was a warm sunny Sunday morning in July. The village church nestled in the centre of a

Chapter 1 – All Change

tiny sleepy village, which didn't boast the luxury of a pub. Outside the church the sheep grazed lazily and the cows lay chewing the cud, a picture of contentment. Through the stillness of the air bird song rang out. It was an idyllic setting for any wedding. Sunday weddings in the village were not an unusual occurrence as it was the centre of a farming community and farmers find it difficult to take leave any day of the week. It was because of Graham's work that a Sunday wedding was ideal; the key members of the firm could attend the wedding, as it was the only day the firm was closed. After the reception Graham and I returned to Birmingham to our new home. The next day saw us both back at work, our honeymoon was delayed until the school holidays when we spent a week afloat on the Norfolk Broads.

I knew married life would not be easy. We were both independent, strong willed people who had been used to living alone in our own homes. Our new life style would need adaptation from both of us. In the early months of our marriage I was happy, but two things gave me cause for concern. Firstly, I didn't like my new home. It was a modern, characterless bungalow situated on a main road between Birmingham and Redditch. We had neighbours I never saw. Secondly, Graham worked long hours and what little spare time he had was spent playing golf. My life seemed to be mundane with teaching, cooking and housework occupying my time. I was facing the danger of becoming bored with resentment setting in. Graham, a sensitive man, knew I was not contented and sought a way to give me a new interest. One October evening Graham brought a present home for me, which would have a far-reaching affect on our lives, although neither of us realized it at the time.

Graham came home early that evening announcing his arrival by screaming at the top of his voice, "Ann, come in to the kitchen. I've got a surprise for you." I walked in to see a large cardboard box placed in the middle of the table. I opened it quickly and to my delight and surprise, curled up in the box was a minute grey kitten.

"Where did you find it?" I asked.

"I was visiting a transport yard this afternoon when I saw some kittens running around. The Foreman told me their resident mouser had given birth to them about eight weeks ago. Of course, they were now becoming a nuisance so they wanted to get rid of them. I thought this little scrap would be company for Charlie and keep you occupied at the same time." As I looked at the tiny form I told Graham "I'll get it out of the box and see if it is a male or female." Without hesitation, I put my hand inside the box to remove the kitten. That was my first mistake! The adorable ball of fur changed in seconds into a tigress, with ears flattened, wide eyed, spitting furiously clawing wildly at my hands. With the experience I have gained over the years I should have known better. This was a feral kitten; it had not been in contact with human beings and wasn't bothered now if it never met one again. I was not going to be beaten by such a small creature. I hung on to the protesting, writhing bundle determined to take a closer look. Amazed, I said to Graham "This isn't a grey kitten, it's covered in oil and filth. We will have to bathe it in case it ingests any of the oil, and poisons itself."

Graham had seen the frenzied kitten in action. The blood was steadily oozing from my lacerated hands covering the table and my clothes. In a voice filled with trepidation he said, "What's with the we? I don't fancy the idea of washing that kitten! It looks pretty mad to me."

"Don't be such a coward," I chided "It's ridiculous a full grown man being afraid of this tiny thing."

The two of us wrestled with the creature, the kitchen resembled a battlefield, soapsuds and water everywhere. We were both soaked but triumphantly I held aloft a wet, bedraggled black and white squeaky-clean kitten. Like all conscientious owners I took the kitten to my local vet for a check up and a course of vaccinations. My vet was an elderly man nearing retirement. He was always very patient with the animals but he had an aversion to being bitten or scratched. As I showed him my latest acquisition he seemed unimpressed with the firebrand in front of him." Where on earth did you find this kitten?" I told him how Graham had come to bring the waif home. In a firm tone he said, " I hope your husband isn't going to make a habit of this. The kitten is obviously feral and treating it is going to be difficult." He wasn't wrong; the kitten seemed to have an inbuilt awareness that this stranger was a vet. With great difficulty he managed to discover the kitten was female, and to vaccinate her. But throughout the consultation, Tuppence as we called her, tried to scratch and bite as much human bare flesh as she could find. I left my vet well and truly scarred from his encounter with Tuppence. I hoped she would

Chapter 1 - All Change

mellow with age or I would need to find another vet! Looking after Tuppence took up a lot of my time, she needed to be convinced that humans were worth knowing. Slowly our firecracker changed into a gentler beast, but she could always suddenly spark into aggression. Unlike Charlie she never sought our company; she preferred to play the Greta Garbo and be alone. As Tuppence grew, the time I needed to devote to her became less, but a seed of an idea had begun to germinate in my brain. I still resented the hours Graham spent playing golf. I didn't have any hobbies. I was a useless sportswoman, and I had no intention of taking up golf. If I was passionate about anything I could admit to being animal crackers. I had enjoyed having a kitten in the house and it seemed the most natural thing in the world to think about breeding cats. I bought some good books and began reading about the wide variety of cat breeds. The more I read the keener I became; all I had to do was to sell the idea to Graham! It took three months of pleading, cajoling, and grovelling but in the end I won my case. By Easter I had bought two female Burmese kittens. The older of the two kittens was a dainty brown Burmese called Chula. Typical of the breed she was very affectionate, mischievous and convinced she was invincible. The younger kitten was a lilac Burmese who we named Ki ie. She was the ladylike one who watched bemused as Chula impersonated Tarzan and swung through the air leaping from curtain to curtain, as we had no jungle vines with which to entertain her! Within weeks Chula spent every spare moment draped around my neck. I did the cooking and washing up with my living fur collar. Ki ie had her moments. She was addicted to sponge cake and baking day was an open invitation for her to steal into the kitchen and nibble the edges of a cake cooling on the rack.

I was a novice breeder thirsty for knowledge; I wanted to learn all I could. From my years of cat breeding I have learnt that there are many people who enter the fancy wanting to breed but it becomes a flight of fancy. The hard work, heartbreak and determination needed are too much for them and they fall by the wayside. I never gave it a thought that I would only breed cats for a couple of years and then move on to something else, nor did I realise that two Burmese kittens would have such a far-reaching affect on my future.

I threw myself into my new hobby with gusto. The phone bill trebled over night as I chatted to cat breeders throughout the UK. I

Life on the Funny Farm

started to understand the importance of pedigrees, and how a certain mating would produce a desired feature in the next generation. I hated Biology at school but now I could be found engrossed in books about genetics. If it wasn't genetics I was studying it was studbooks, looking for the right mate for my girls.

When I purchased Ki ie the breeder had entered her for a show and I agreed I would take her. I didn't realise it then but it was to be the start of a long association with showing. I would experience the highs of success and the troughs of despondency but nevertheless kept on going. I remember little about that first show except Ki ie won her open class. I was thrilled and my enthusiasm knew no bounds. The rosette we won I still have to this day. It has a place of pride in my trophy cabinet although it appears a little dog-eared around the edges. Still reeling from the heady success of my first show I decided to enter more. I couldn't wait for the next show day.

Life was good, I enjoyed my job, I had found a hobby which enthralled me, and soon we were going to celebrate our first wedding anniversary. I could not have been happier or more content, when a bombshell was dropped into my cosy little existence. During the summer I had not felt well. The dizzy spells continued and I was worried enough to visit my doctor. The diagnosis was quick and simple, a common ailment – I was pregnant! It came as a huge shock, Graham was delighted, over the moon but I felt suicidal! I knew this was the end of my career as I had known it. My plans for a family were in the distant future, not here and now. I wasn't at all sure how I would cope with being a mother and all the adjustments I would have to make. I suddenly faced my future with trepidation.

Life had to go on. I had entered more cat shows and by now even an idiot could tell I was pregnant; at the next show I attended a friend shouted out across a crowded bar, "I hope the stud had a top quality pedigree."

I replied flippantly, "Definitely, and the litter is due early January."

I cancelled all my future shows, as I grew larger and larger resembling a landed whale. A month before my baby was born, I had another shock; it wasn't one, but twins! I knew then I would not return to teaching; I could not see how I could look after two babies and fit in a career. However, I knew I would need something other than the

Chapter 1 - All Change

babies to occupy me. I was going to be tied to the children. My four cats already restricted my freedom, so why not embark on an even more tying occupation and run a boarding cattery? I put the idea to Graham who agreed. When the children were born we would look for a suitable property where we could build a cattery.

The day arrived at the beginning of January when I was admitted to hospital for the birth of my twins. I was blessed with a healthy boy and girl whom we named Joe and Lucy. Only four minutes separated their births and as the years rolled by, it has become the most contested four minutes in their lives. From the minute they were born all my fears and doubts vanished as I looked down on the two helpless forms. My maternal instincts flowed through my body; there was no woman in the maternity wing prouder or happier than I.

The babies grew; my feline family had accepted these pink wriggly arrivals with no trouble at all. I settled into the routine of feeding, nappy changing and with twins there was little time left for anything else. The daffodils coming into bloom heralded the arrival of spring. It was also accompanied by the raucous calling of my two adult Burmese cats whose thoughts had turned to flights of sexual fantasies. Anyone who has ever owned an entire female cat can bear witness to the banshee wails produced constantly day and night as they try to attract a mate. It was decision time – was I going to give up cat breeding before I had started or mate the girls?

Chapter 2
To Be Or Not To Be?

The answer was simple; to stud they would go, packed with blankets and treats, each girl set off for her steamy rendezvous with nature. I have already mentioned some members of my family but I have failed to introduce my parents. My father, Tom, was a handsome, slightly built man but he had a big personality, and a heart to match. For as long as I can remember he had been keenly interested in animals. In my early years, he taught me about chickens, rabbits, rodents and even locusts. He had a natural empathy with animals and had always encouraged me. At one time in his life he seriously considered farming as a career, but the Second World War put a stop to that ambition. Instead, after the war he trained as a teacher, and used his considerable organisational skills to rise to the post of Headmaster. He was an authoritative figure despite his slight frame, he effortlessly managed to command the respect of all who knew him. My mother too, was slightly built. She had a great sense of humour, was intelligent, very caring and supported my father whole heartedly in everything he chose to do. One of my earliest recollections as a child is sitting in the kitchen watching my mother cook. She readily admitted when she married Tom that she could only boil an egg. She taught herself culinary skills, and consequently found cooking an absorbing hobby. Typical of her generation, she was an expert homemaker. I owe my interest and ability to cook to Emily's tuition. The same can not be said about sewing and knitting, at both of which my mother excelled, unlike her daughter who struggles to re-

Chapter 2 - To be or not to be?

place a button!   Sometimes she found it difficult to understand my passion for animals and was known to accuse my father of encouraging me to expand my animal family. My mother grew up by the seaside in Norfolk and according to tales I heard from my grandmother, she was forever rescuing kittens and puppies that had been thrown into the harbour in sacks to drown. Whether they like it or not, both Tom and Emily are both equally responsible for my love of animals. You can not choose your parents, and I doubt if I had been given a choice, I could have done better. They have always loved me no matter what, supported me regardless, and have always been there for me. So it was no surprise that they would become involved in my hobby.   The girls had a wonderful time with their respective husbands and it was time for them to return home. My father volunteered to fetch Chula back from her honeymoon. My mother went along for the ride. I shall never forget the sight of the two of them when they arrived home with Chula. Tom's face was ashen and my mother was trembling.

"Let me make you a cup of tea, you look as though you could do with one," I offered.

Emily still shaking in a strained voice said, " Tea! I need a whisky."

This really was a cause for concern for my mother's only tipple was usually a glass of stout.

"That cat," began my father, "has screamed incessantly all of the fifty miles home. When it wasn't screaming it was clawing maniacally at the carrier trying to escape. Your mother was yelling at me to drive faster so we could reach here sooner. You can tell how horrendous it all was, even travelling at seventy miles an hour didn't cause your mother to object.".

Could my dad really be telling the truth? For mum any speed over forty is excessive! One look at their faces confirmed the truth of what they were saying. To prove how magnanimous they were, the future would see them driving half the breadth of the country with more protesting girls in the back, but the first time is always the worst or so they say!

The weeks went by and both girls were pregnant, nine weeks after their amours our household was about to swell in numbers. I was ready for the event. I had prepared a kittening box, Graham had stated categorically at the beginning that no cat was going to give birth in our bedroom, so I prepared the spare room. Reminiscent of my teaching days I had devised a series of wall charts illustrating every presentation of a kitten at birth known to veterinary science. I had left nothing to chance. As the time approached I moved into the room with the girls, deserting my husband. Graham was far from pleased that I should choose to sleep with a cat in preference to him, but he bore it stoically. Unknown to Graham this was a glimpse of the future, something he still finds irksome to this day.

Ki ie gave birth first, not in my beautiful, purpose-built, no expense spared kittening box, but on my pillow. Ki ie strained to deliver the first kitten and eventually one foot appeared. I am ashamed to admit I fell to pieces, this wasn't on any of my wall charts. I concluded it had to be a problem delivery. I knew exactly what to do, it was now two a.m. I ran into our bedroom and shook Graham's sleeping form violently.

I shrieked, "Come quick. Ki ies having a kitten and it's all going wrong."

Graham stumbled out of bed and lumbered in a sleepy daze towards the spare room muttering, "I don't know what you expect me to do.".

When we reached the room we saw Ki ie draped contentedly across the pillow with a live, healthy but very wet kitten crawling along her stomach searching for the milk bar!

"Well I'm no expert but that cat doesn't look to be in much trouble to me. If you have no objections I'm going back to bed and maybe I will get some sleep." The exasperation was clear in his voice and as he trundled back to bed I settled down with Ki ie.

Ki ie continued in labour throughout the night and as daylight dawned she had given birth to eight beautiful, healthy babies. The whole experience had worried me to death, but during the day I kept wandering in to peek at the new family. It gave me a wonderful feeling, nature at its very best. Even to this day witnessing the birth of a litter of kittens fills me with wonder.

The next evening, I took Chula to bed with me but not before Graham uttered this dire warning, " Don't think about waking me tonight; you wanted to do this breeding lark so don't drag me into it, especially in the middle of the night. I've got a big day at work to-

Chapter 2 – To be or not to be?

morrow, I need to be fresh and alert." I assured him that I wouldn't lose my nerve again, and I happily settled down to play midwife.

Chula appreciated my efforts and gave birth to her litter in the designer kitten box. All was going well, Chula was giving birth to her kittens like shelling peas, they were coming fast and furious. The fourth kitten born seemed lifeless; I began rubbing the tiny form vigorously but to little effect. When the fifth kitten was born, that too did not appear to be very enthusiastic about life. I just hadn't got enough pairs of hands to tend to them both, the solution was blindingly clear. At three o clock in the morning I rushed into our bedroom clutching the lifeless form.

"Wake up Graham," I shouted as I shook Graham until he woke. " Keep rubbing this kitten.".

Graham opened his bleary eyes as I thrust the wet, cold kitten into his hands. I didn't wait for a reply as I rushed back to Chula who was now giving birth to kitten number six. When the crisis was over I returned sheepishly to our bedroom. Graham sat on the edge of the bed nursing a wriggling, protesting kitten. Before I could shower him with thanks and praise he looked up at me through his bloodshot eyes and through clenched teeth muttered, "Don't you ever do that to me again." To this day, I never have, I wouldn't dare!

In a matter of forty-eight hours our cat population had increased by fifteen; over the weeks rearing the kittens brought me great joy, but I was soon to have other things on my mind. We still planned to move and open a boarding cattery; we spent spare moments viewing properties but none were suitable despite all the agents' jargon. One Sunday we arranged to view a property in the countryside beside a lake. It sounded ideal, but like all the others we had seen it wasn't suitable. Both of us were deflated, as we drove home it seemed as though we were searching for the impossible. As we drove along Graham pointed to a bungalow which stood alone, surrounded by fields.

"That's the type of place we need," no sooner had Graham spoken than he slammed on the brakes. By the gate was a board boldly stating: FOR SALE. I didn't need Graham to say a word, I wrote down the agent's details and at nine o clock the next morning I rang them. We arranged a viewing for that afternoon.

Chapter 3
The End of a Quest

The bungalow stood in one acre of gardens and had a further eight acres of land with it. The green lawns were well kept, and immaculate flower borders surrounded the house. There was a large vegetable garden, it was clear that someone had tended the garden with loving care. Some yards from the house was a stable block and yard; there were other various outbuildings, which included a barn, tack room and poultry house. The owner had been an elderly gentleman who had died suddenly. His daughter did not want to keep the farm so she had put it on the market. As soon as I walked through the gate, my love affair with the farm began.

The bungalow itself had been neglected, it would need a lot more than a good clean and a coat of paint to set it right. The house in which we were living was modern; it could almost be classed as luxurious. The farm, on the other hand, seemed to have stepped straight from the 1950's. There was no fitted kitchen just an old cooker, a cracked ceramic sink and a few cupboards scattered haphazardly around the walls. Leading from the kitchen was a conservatory but a better description would have been a lean to. The bathroom was no better, the décor was black and white, some tiles were missing others were cracked. The bath was stained brown; it would not have looked out of place in a field as a water trough! The three bedrooms were drab with no fitted wardrobes just four plain walls. The lounge was something else. It was a huge room with a plain red brick fireplace at

Chapter 3 – The End of a Quest

one end. Like the rest of the house it was dreary, dirty but that room sold the bungalow to me. I imagined how it could be with an archway; recessed lighting and a roaring log fire in the grate. I knew if we bought it, there would be a lot of hard work ahead, but the struggles would be worth it. When Graham saw the bungalow, he said only one word sprang to mind.

"Hovel!" However, Graham saw a business opportunity. He is a man of vision and realised that this drab bungalow could be turned into a comfortable home and a new venture.

The next morning, we rang the agents and made an offer, and then we waited. The farm was in my thoughts constantly throughout the week. I began to think about all the new avenues we could explore if we were fortunate to move there. The poultry house would be ideal to house a flock of free-range hens. It was the beginning of 1980, the country was gripped by a recession and we would need a bridging loan if we bought the farm. Any income we could earn from the farm would be a great help. The fields and the stables could bring in much needed revenue as it would be sometime before we could open a cattery. I also realised I would have no near neighbours and this meant that while I was alone during the day I would be vulnerable. My birthday was fast approaching and Graham had asked if there was anything in particular I would like. I had my request ready, I wanted a puppy. Graham wasn't enamoured with the idea as the animal contingent of our household was relentlessly expanding. If we acquired the farm, a dog was essential.

A week passed by, and I continued to make plans but we heard nothing from the agents. I was beginning to fear that I would have to face bitter disappointment, when the shrill ringing of the phone cut into my thoughts. I answered the phone and heard Graham's familiar voice. "Ann, I've heard from the estate agents, they have received three serious offers for the farm. We are all being given an opportunity to improve our offers."

My heart was thumping, the adrenalin was flowing. I really wanted the farm but not at any price. My head ruled my heart as I replied,

"You know I would offer anything if I thought it would secure the sale for us, but you know what we can afford so it's your decision."

Life on the Funny Farm

"I'll decide on a figure and notify the agents. They said they would give us their decision today. Once I hear anything I will ring you; meantime, keep your fingers crossed, love." The phone went dead as Graham replaced the receiver and I was left with a turmoil of
emotions. I couldn't settle to anything, I hovered around the phone waiting, but the day slowly wore on and still there was no word. As the time approached five o'clock, at long last the phone rang. With great trepidation, I hesitantly picked up the receiver to hear Graham's exuberant voice booming down the line, "Ann we've got it, the farm's all ours." I was thrilled, over the moon; the fact that a lot of hard work was ahead of me could not dampen my spirits. I waited eagerly for Graham's return so we could discuss our plans for the future. I thought it wise not to mention my idea about chickens but I had not forgotten my birthday present!

Eventually, Graham returned home. The evening was spent making plans, both of us excited at the prospect of a new challenge. We discussed a plan of work, which we hoped would enable us to move into the farm within three months. Very gently, I raised the subject of security.

"I've been thinking living out in the country with no neighbours, we ought to have a dog about the place. It would make me feel safer when you are at work.".

Graham has always known when he is beaten and gives in graciously. This time was no exception. I decided I would wait a couple of days before I told him I had located an adorable Golden Retriever puppy. Perhaps it wasn't a typical breed of guard dog but it would make a super addition to our family.

As we lay in bed that night I was happy beyond measure, I had a new home to look forward to and sooner than Graham realised, a puppy in the house. I was so excited sleep eluded me, thoughts rushed through my mind, churning over the events of the day. Curious, I asked, "Graham how did you decide your final offer for the farm?"

Graham answered, "I wrote three sets of figures on to separate pieces of paper. The lowest figure I thought would be acceptable, the highest the most we could afford, and a figure in between the two. Having done that I put the papers into a hat and asked my secretary

Chapter 3 - The End of a Quest

to pull one out. The figure she drew out was my final offer." I listened with disbelief, how relieved I was that I had not known our future was being left to a game of chance.

Chapter 4
The In-Laws

For the next four months we spent every spare moment preparing for the move. Each day I would pack my car with the twins and all their paraphernalia, plus our puppy called Sally and set off the short distance to the farm. Once there, I unloaded the car and settled the children into their bouncy chairs. I began to paint the rooms and clean the house from top to bottom. Mum and Dad arrived in their touring caravan set-up camp on the drive and helped with decorating. Towards the end of September the bungalow was as ready as it ever would be to move into.

My in-laws Fred and Rose looked after the twins on the day we actually moved. I set off long before the removal van arrived, with Sally, four cats and two kittens. By the time the furniture arrived at the farm the animals were safely settled. It was a long, hard day, Graham could not leave work so I had to direct operations alone. Finally, at six o'clock everything was in place. We fetched the twins and settled down to a quiet night in, relaxing in our new home.

After a good night's sleep, we awoke early the next morning ready to do battle. Graham climbed out of bed and pressed the light switch but nothing happened. Irritably, he said, "Wonderful! The bulbs have blown, where are the spares?"

I hadn't a clue which box they were in but most of the boxes were in the kitchen so I decided to make a cup of tea and search in the meantime. I turned the light on in the kitchen but nothing

Chapter 4 – The In-Laws

happened. Slowly it dawned on me that we had a total power failure. The only source of power in the bungalow was electricity; without it our oil fired central heating cannot work. We rang the emergency power number and we were informed a tree had fallen onto the overhead power lines. They were trying to solve the problem but they had no idea when power would be restored. Graham was always resourceful and immediately employed the Dunkirk spirit.

"I'll light a fire and we can at least have some toast. Whilst I'm doing that, Ann, you can make up a couple of bottles for the kids and we will warm them over the fire."

Having received my instructions, I got to work. We did manage the toast but the children's plastic bottles began to melt in the heat from the fire. There was no alternative but to call the cavalry – the cavalry, being the in-laws.

My father-in-law, Fred, was a larger than life character. He was a self-made man who had battled through life to fulfil his dream to have his own firm. He was short in stature, with an ample waistline which bore testimony to his love of good food and wine. He was proud of his humble origins, one of a large family, born and bred in the terraced streets of Birmingham. Life was hard but it helped to shape his character. He had certainly seen life, not least, when as a young man he ran away to join the circus. Eventually, he became a lorry driver, and tried working for others. Slowly he built his own transport business. He had a love for dogs, particularly Greyhounds, which he trained and owned. Over the years, he bred many winners, and his hard won trophies had a place of pride in his lounge. A favourite pastime for Fred was a day at the races, he would have liked to own his own racehorse, but Rose would have none of it. My mother-in-law, Rose was very down to earth, and was quick to point out that fast women and slow horses have been the ruin of many a good man. Like Fred she was brought up in the city, one of eight daughters, all of whom had striking titian coloured hair. Like Emily, she supported her husband in every way. She was not animal minded, the countryside was a complete mystery to her. An even bigger mystery for her was why her son chose to marry a woman who, over the years, has surrounded herself with animals of all shapes and sizes. Rose accepted, where animals were concerned we would beg to differ, but when the chips were down she could always be relied on to turn up trumps! This is exactly what they did.

Within an hour Fred and Rose arrived with a large gas camping stove, at last we could feed the twins. Things didn't seem so bad. The day wore on but still we had no power. By the afternoon Graham was becoming mutinous, his Dunkirk spirit was waning, "I must have been mad to let you talk me into moving here, I don't even like the countryside, to think of the home we left with all mod cons, now look at us." I tried to smooth his ruffled feathers.

"They will get the power back on soon and then we will laugh about all this." The power did not return. Instead, things were about to get worse! Graham went to fill the kettle and his irate yell echoed around the room.

"Ann, there's no water coming out of the tap." For a moment I couldn't understand why we should have no water then realisation dawned. The bungalow is not connected to mains water. Our water is extracted from a borehole and an electric pump brings the water to the surface. Our sewage is stored in a septic tank which is emptied on a regular basis.

This wasn't how I had envisaged our first day in our new home. We sat huddled together in one room with the coal fire our only warmth. As dusk began to fall, the light from the fire and candles gave the room a romantic air but the atmosphere was decidedly chilly as Graham and I sat in strained silence. Finally, just before we retired to bed the power was restored. As a child, I had enjoyed the occasional power cut but I felt traumatised by this experience. It was one we would not forget. Over the years we have experienced numerous power failures, the overhead lines are very susceptible to damage, but now we are well prepared with a generator which can at least ensure we have a supply of running water. I always have an endless supply of candles, a powerful torch, a portable gas stove and heater. Our first day at the farm taught us a lesson we would not forget.

Chapter 5
Making Ends Meet

Graham and I put into action our plan to fund our bridging loan, whilst the cattery was being built we would receive an income from the stables. I placed an advertisement in the local paper and hoped we would be inundated with people wishing to stable their horses with us. My father had worked with horses many years earlier and gave me these words of caution, "Remember the front-end bites and the back-end kicks!" He wasn't far wrong. To my relief we had too many applicants for the nine stables we had available. Farmers are reluctant to let horses graze on their land as they cause damage to the fields and this meant stabling was at a premium.

Within two weeks all the stables had been let. We offered a part livery service, this entailed being responsible for letting the horses out in the morning and in the colder months rugging them up. My father-in-law, Fred, was quick to voice his concern

"I don't like the idea of you handling all those horses on your own, what if you had an accident? No one would know."

I had always liked horses and as a child had pestered my parents to let me own a pony but financially it had not been possible. I didn't realise as a child how much it cost to keep a horse. It is said a horse costs as much as a car to maintain and that is a fair assessment. I patiently explained to Fred, "We need the money, we don't have a choice. I'm sure everything will be alright."

Fred sternly said in a tone that left no room for argument, "I appreciate the financial need, if you insist on doing it then I shall come over each morning and help you rug them up and turn them out."

Fred did exactly that for many months and I must admit there were hair raising moments, when I was only too glad he was with me.

Most of the horses we stabled were owned by schoolgirls, the largest horse was called Percy. He was a chestnut thoroughbred standing seventeen hands high. As I am just under five feet tall, he looked a very big horse to me. He was a good natured horse, which was just as well because I found it very difficult to lift his rug onto his back, I just wasn't tall enough. Fred solved the problem by producing a solid wooden soapbox for me to stand on.

Some of the horses we stabled were difficult and mean natured, but I soon discovered horses moved between stable yards frequently and usually the horses I liked least stayed for only a short while. One of the first horses to arrive was a part Arab bay mare, just fifteen hands high called Fleur. Unlike most of the others she was owned by a mature lady. I didn't realise it then but Fleur was to become part of the fixtures and fittings on the farm and her owner Jenny became a very dear friend.

Now we had an income from the farm Graham and I began to draw up the plans for the cattery. We applied to the local council for permission to erect sixteen cat pens, this was a slow laborious process. The council were none too keen, as there was already a number of boarding establishments in the area, and not all of them had a good reputation. I had to convince them I was only interested in running a cattery of the highest standard. It took many letters and meetings but finally they agreed in principle. We heard of a cattery in Surrey, the owners were retiring and had offered their cat houses for sale. Graham sent one of his lorries to collect them. We had secured them at a bargain price but they needed a great deal of work to improve them. My uncle who lives locally agreed to help refurbish them but we needed to build runs to attach to them. My father stepped into the breach and volunteered to make the runs. Tom is a perfectionist, and any task he performs is executed to the utmost degree of professionalism. Our aim was to complete six pens and have them operational by the following May, just in time for the holiday season.

Chapter 5 – Making Ends Meet

As I waited for the cattery to be built, my days began to follow a set pattern. I could begin to concentrate on my hobby again. I had not attended a cat show for over a year, it was time to get back into circulation. I entered the Midland Cat Show which was to be held in November. I had kept a blue Burmese kitten from my first litter, she was a pretty cat which I named Bluebell. I decided to take her to the show. This was the first cat of my own breeding, which I had shown. The twins were too young to go with me so my mother agreed to look after them for the day. I set off for the show with my cousin in tow to keep me company. The show was held at the very new National Exhibition Centre in Birmingham. Our class was a large one but Bluebell looked a picture and won her open and Best of Breed. I was elated but a breeder of many years came to me and said, "It's beginners luck, enjoy it while you can."

I shrugged off her comment, but how right she was, it would be over a year before I would win an open again!

I had settled into my new home and could not have been happier. At my previous house I had not known my neighbours as they were out at work all day, and now I had none. I wondered how I would meet the local people.

Chapter 6
The Villagers

As I was out and about with the children I began to meet the villagers. In a small community there is an infallible grapevine of what's going on in the locality. I was viewed as an incomer, the villagers were curious about our plans for the farm. Within a short space of time it seemed that everyone knew who I was and I had been labelled, "the cat woman of Wyckam." Once their fears were allayed, that we had no plans to develop the farm other than for housing animals, we were accepted into the community.

Our nearest neighbour is one hundred and fifty yards away and they live over the Saddlery shop, which they own. They moved into the village about the same time as we. They sell animal feeds as well as equestrian accessories so my visits were frequent. When we bought the farm neither Graham nor I knew anything about managing grassland but I soon realised that our fields would need some expert attention if they were to continue to supply grazing for horses. On one of my visits to the Saddlery, I enquired if they knew of any agricultural contractors. I pointed out that I knew nothing so I needed someone whom I could trust and who would charge a fair rate for the work done. On a piece of paper, a name and telephone number were scribbled and when I got home I rang the number and asked to speak to Bert. He agreed to meet me and said he would visit at a time convenient for him.

It was some days before I met Bert, in fact I began to wonder if he would come at all. I soon discovered that Bert did things in his own

Chapter 6 – The Villagers

time. When Bert arrived my first impression was of a man who had never heard of Saville Row, he wore a flat cap rammed tightly onto his head, his trousers were ill fitting held up by a piece of bright orange bailing twine. His shirt had seen plenty of wear, he portrayed the image of a man down on his luck. Bert brought with him a younger man, his farm hand, who was so similar it was a double act. I explained what I thought needed doing and Bert surveyed the land. He came back to me and slowly tipped his cap forward, revealing fine wisps of hair; he proceeded to scratch his head as if deep in thought. "Well, Anna, the fields need harrowing and rolling, and then we will muck spread."

"Do whatever you think is needed, how much will it cost? By the way, my name is Ann."

"I'll do the job in the next few days. Anna, you can pay me then."

With that they left the farm. I was to learn that Bert never quoted for a job but over the years I have always found him to be very fair. Bert has always called me Anna, I have never bothered to correct him again. From that first meeting I could not know that Bert would become my mentor as he encouraged me to keep farming livestock. Over the years he was to become a friend, a rock in times of crisis, and a man I respected for his honesty and courage.

Some days later, Bert arrived with the tractors and began work. He never seemed to start before noon and by one o'clock he went home for lunch. He returned an hour later only to down tools at half past three so he could collect his many children from school. Sometimes he would work for a while longer depending on the season of the year. However, the job would always be completed. Bert was never in a hurry to present his bill either. Sometimes I was short of funds, this never worried Bert. He would characteristically tip his cap forward, scratch his head, ponder a moment and quietly say, "That's all right, Anna. Pay me when you can."

By now Ki ie, my Burmese had given birth to her second litter but things were not straight forward, some of the kittens were sickly and failed to thrive. I was now more knowledgeable about pedigrees, and Ki ie had a number of cats in her ancestry which had produced breeding problems. I decided to spay Ki ie and find good homes for the kittens that survived. By chance, a lady called Mary who lived locally came to see me and fell in love with one of the kittens. She decided

Life on the Funny Farm

she would take her home. During our conversation she told me about her job. The farm we had bought was surrounded by battery chicken farms. Mary's job was to rear the chicks to be housed at the farms. I always planned to have chickens and so I asked her where I could get some. She told me not to worry as she had plenty who were injured or damaged and she would bring them to me. She was as good as her word and within days eighteen shell-shocked hens arrived.

Chapter 7
Feathered Friends

The motley crew of hens did look a sorry sight. They all had few feathers and some had wounds where they had been pecked in the cages by stronger birds. They all found walking difficult, as there is little room in a cage, they had paid dearly so the consumer could have cheap eggs. The first few weeks I only let them out if the weather conditions were kind, but gradually their strength was renewed and they began to behave, as birds should, scratching the ground, enjoying dust baths. I was rewarded by a steady supply of eggs. They laid so well we had more eggs than we could eat. One morning as I was collecting the eggs one of the girls who kept her horse with us came to chat to me and I offered her some eggs to take home. She was pleased but asked, "How long do we have to leave the eggs in the fridge before we can eat them?"

I was amazed at such a question but nevertheless told her she could eat a new laid egg quite safely, it didn't have to stand on a supermarket shelf for days before it was edible! My small flock of hens were happy and contented but their happiness would know no bounds after Mary's latest visit. Mary called in one afternoon to give me a progress report on her kitten, her hand was tightly clutching a sack.

"What's in the sack?" I asked.

"I thought this might come in useful, sometimes the chicks are wrongly sexed and then as they grow we realise we have a cockerel on our hands. They are no use in a battery house". She opened the sack and out leapt a handsome cream and brown rooster. I took him straight away to meet his harem but much to my dismay they were not impressed. In fact, they set about him. However, it did not take them long to accept him and he guarded his girls jealously. I had not named any of the hens but I felt this magnificent male should be given a title. Years ago, I read a mythical creation story about a cockerel who had awakened the world. He was named Chanteclere and so our rooster became known as Chantey.

Graham was quite pleased that we had a flock of hens as he enjoyed the eggs, which they produced. Hens are not the most intelligent creatures but they soon learnt when I whistled it meant it was suppertime and they would come running from all corners of the farm for their food. Although they roamed free during the day at night they were confined to the hen house to protect them from the marauding fox. With the hens installed, I began to wonder how I could persuade Graham to agree to let me have some geese. I had read that geese made wonderful watchdogs and as I had predicted, our Golden Retriever was a marvellous addition to our family, but as a guard, left a lot to be desired. To my surprise, Graham had no objections to geese on the farm so I quickly scanned the ads and bought three geese. I bought a gander and two geese. They were completely white and had a majestic air.

For the first couple of days I kept them confined to the yard area and then allowed them complete freedom on the farm. They were young geese but fully-grown. Soon after their arrival, I was working outside on the farm when I noticed the cars passing the farm were slowing down. This is quite common, as often there are horses and riders using the road. I was unperturbed until the cars began to sound their horns. Something was wrong; no one in their right mind would use their car horn near a horse. I decided to go and investigate. As I peered over the gate, in the distance I could see three small white heads bobbing up and down in the centre of the road. The geese with their peculiar gait were imitating the Egyptian Sand Dancers. I wondered how the geese had got out! Without a moment's delay I rushed after them. I managed to stop the traffic and then get ahead of them and turn them around. Slowly, they began to waddle back home. The car drivers were getting impatient but one driver asked if he could help. I accepted his offer of help gratefully. All was going

Chapter 7 - Feathered Friends

well until forty yards from home when one of the geese decided to break away and seek refuge in a deep ditch, which surrounds our property. I had no option but to climb into the ditch myself and capture the goose. The driver who was helping me followed to the edge of the ditch. By now, I had the goose tucked tightly under my arm. He said, "Pass the duck to me and then you will be able to climb out yourself."

"Thank you for helping, by the way it isn't a duck, it's a goose."

In a voice full of authority he said, "I'm not holding any goose, they bite you know."

Before I knew what was happening, the man had gone and I was still stuck in the ditch with the goose. I did manage to get the goose home eventually but it taught me a lesson; from now on if people thought they were ducks so be it, I wasn't going to enlighten them.

The geese have never strayed from the farm since. Over the years they have been excellent watchers and terrorised family, friends and visitors alike. On a summer's day, they sit motionless on the lawn basking in the sun with a regal air, customers still think they are big ducks. Some even think they are swans, I leave them happy in their ignorance.

Christmas was fast approaching, the cattery was slowly being built and I was so busy there were not enough hours in the day. We decided I would advertise for a cleaning lady to help two mornings a week. Money was still in short supply but my mother insisted on paying her wages. I put a card in the local Post Office and within hours I received a telephone call from a lady called Doris. Doris came for an interview. She was a small, stocky built lady in her early sixties. Her hands and face bore the evidence of a lifetime of gruelling work. She had raised a large family of her own, and now in later life she had been recruited into helping rear her grandchildren. A toothless smile energised her abundant facial wrinkles into movement. She had a motherly appearance and I warmed to her immediately. Doris was the type of lady who would have to work hard all her life to grub a living, she was the salt of the earth and I had no hesitation in offering her the job. She told me she already 'did' for another person, so two mornings would suit her fine. Typical of her generation, she did a wonderful cleaning job and within weeks she volunteered to help with my ironing, she was an angel! There was just one problem – Doris was terrified of the geese. I don't know what it is about animals but they can always sense fear and geese are no different. The geese seemed instinctively aware which days of the week Doris worked and they would stand guard by the gate. At first she would try and outrun them but they were too quick and would hang from the hem of her skirt. Doris devised her own strategy she arrived with bread and would hurl this over the gate. The geese would devour it greedily, by which time Doris had reached the sanctuary of the porch. This plan of action worked for a couple of weeks but the geese were not to be thwarted. Patiently, they lay in wait for Doris to finish work and she would have to run the gauntlet to the gate. I feared Doris would resign but she was made of sterner stuff. The solution was simple, she doubled her bread supplies and saved half for the sprint out of the farm!

The winter months made life hard on the farm, the freezing weather meant the outside water taps froze, the animals' water buckets were solid ice, and every job took longer and it was more difficult to remain cheerful. The ground was frozen rock solid so the horses remained in their stables. During the day I had to make sure they had fresh hay and water. Some of the owners left bucket feeds, which I distributed amongst them. The hens and geese found the winter a trial, reluctant to venture out from their houses. In their protest, our supply of new laid eggs dried up. At last, I could see the shoots of snowdrops pushing through the frozen ground heralding the end of winter.

Chapter 8
Spring Brings a New Life

The early spring saw the arrival of lorries laden with ready mixed concrete to lay the base for the cattery. The weather was kind to us and the concrete went off quickly. All we needed now was the pens to be completed. I made all the vets in the locality aware that we would soon be opening a cattery but an advert in the Yellow Pages could not be included until the following year. My uncle and Tom, completed their work on time. Graham erected the houses and runs, we were open for business. Slowly the enquiries came and our first feline guests arrived.

It did not take me long to discover what an awesome responsibility running a cattery can be. Owners leave one of their most treasured belongings in my care, the act of parting reducing some to tears. I believe that most of the animals I look after present few problems. I wish I could say that about the two legged animals which bring them! No book I have ever read about operating a cattery could prepare me for some of the situations I would have to face.

Spring also saw the arrival of yet another addition to the farm. We decided to buy more hens as we found we could sell our surplus eggs easily from the farm gate. I decided to visit a local market where they sold small livestock. Graham was concerned I would buy too many so he commandeered his mother to go with me to curb my enthusiasm. We set off on the Wednesday morning with the twins in the rear of the car. There were all types of hens for sale and Rose began to worry that my enthusiasm would run away with me. As we walked along the pens I was amazed to see a kid goat amongst all the poultry. It was a week old nanny kid. I put my fingers in the cage and she suckled from them immediately, I was smitten.

"Rose, look at this kid. Isn't she just adorable?" I saw grim determination on her face as she said, "Yes, it is very nice but you can't possibly think about buying it. What would Graham say?"

"Oh, don't worry about that. I'll sort it out, he won't mind." I couldn't hide the doubt in my voice.

"You will have to bid for her in the auction, she might be more than you can afford." Rose was clutching at straws hoping against hope I would be out bid.

The auction took place and for the princely sum of four pounds fifty pence I acquired my first goat. We set off for home with the kid sat proudly on Rose's lap. It was a quiet journey home. I was wondering how I was going to break the news to Graham and Rose was mystified how she had become involved in another of her daughter-in-law's hair-brained schemes.

On our return home, Graham rang to find out if we had been successful at the market. My courage had now deserted me and I said I would tell him all when he got home. In the meantime, I busied myself preparing a stable for the kid. I rushed to the farm supply shop and bought dried ewe's milk plus a book all about goat keeping. Before Graham arrived home I had read enough of the book to be able to make a strong case why no farm should be without a goat. Finally, Graham arrived home.

"Come on then, love. Let's have a look at the new hens, I know you're pleased with them because you wouldn't tell me anything about them. I suppose they are a special breed and knowing you they were a bargain."

I took Graham to the stable block, "Why have you put them in here?"

I opened the stable door and the little kid came running to meet me.

"What the hell is that?" he exclaimed.

"It's a nanny kid. Just think when she is older we can have our own milk and cheese. She will be able to graze on the lawn so you won't have to mow it so often."

Chapter 8 – Spring Brings a New Life

"I'd rather have to mow the lawn. You know nothing about goats. Whatever possessed you?"

"I couldn't resist her; she is a little angel. She won't be any bother and I'm not asking you to look after her."

Graham demanded, "What did my mother have to say about this?"

"Not much, she nursed her on her knee all the way home." I studied Graham's face and saw stony disbelief; even his mother had betrayed him!

Graham stalked back to the house shouting, "Where is this all going to end? That's what I would like to know." Fortunately, he had no idea what was in store!

I gave the kid a hug; my little angel had no idea of the rumpus her arrival had caused. I knew Graham would come round in time but I knew it was going to be another evening of strained silence. As I closed the stable door I looked back at the angelic kid and decided she should be called Angie. Angie settled into her new home. There was never a shortage of volunteers to bottle feed her, even Graham was charmed by her. She sought human company and shadowed our every move. Clearly, she was lonely she needed a companion!

Chapter 9
The Art of Kiddology

Angie had only been with us a few days when I noticed two small bony growths protruding from her head. These would develop in time into a set of horns. This gave me a cause for concern; with horns even in play she could become a danger to Lucy and Joe. The children were beginning to take their first tentative steps, and showed childish delight in all the animals around us. There was only one thing to be done; Angie would have to be dehorned. The vet I had used for many years was about to retire, besides which, he did not treat farm animals so it seemed the perfect time to find a vet who ran a mixed practice. There was a surgery only a mile away. I booked Angie an appointment and together we met the new vet.

He was in his early thirties, not a tall man but he had pleasant features and a perfect bedside manner. Neville, as he was called, was charm personified. He treated Angie kindly and I had no worries when I left her in his care. Later that day, I collected her. She was no worse for wear but she had been disbudded. I knew she would not be able to harm the twins, they could grow up and play happily together but it would be a while before Joe and Lucy could be her playmates.

The solution to Angie's friendless state was solved by chance. An acquaintance of mine kept goats and she offered to give me an elderly milking nanny called Susie. I spoke to Graham and he agreed we should have another goat. The first problem we encountered was Susie lived fifty miles away. Graham borrowed one of the vans from work and one weekend we set off to fetch her.

Chapter 9 – The Art of Kiddology

Susie was an older version of Angie, a pure white goat. Her owners told me she was accustomed to being milked from the right hand side standing on a milking box. I was a little more prepared for Susie's arrival and Graham had already made me a milking box. I had read all about milking goats and had practiced on the fingers of an inflated rubber glove. The book had also advised that when learning to milk it was essential to get a rhythm, and singing a good marching tune was a great help. I was confident I would be able to milk her, but first we had to get her home! Susie jumped into the van without a backward glance. We trundled along the country lanes, Susie enjoying every minute. I sat in the passenger seat, Susie was in the rear. I held onto her lead, whilst Graham drove. Susie craned her neck forward so she could watch the scenery passing by, and I talked quietly to her so she would not become perturbed. Within a short while we reached the M6 motorway and the van began to gather speed, we should be home within the hour. Then all hell broke loose, Susie was not a fan of motorways! Susie became agitated and tried to climb on to the passenger seat.

Graham snapped, "Ann you have got to keep her still, otherwise she will be in the front of the van."

Irritably, I replied, "I'm trying to keep her still, but it's not easy!" I wrapped the lead tighter round my hand and tried to soothe her nerves. Nothing was going to calm her.

When animals are afraid they usually lose control of their bowel and bladder, Susie was no exception a loud hissing noise filled the van.

"What's that goat doing in the back?" asked Graham.

"She's having a wee." I saw no point in lying to Graham, the evidence would be visible when we reached home.

Graham was indignant, "She can't do that in my van.".

"Well, she has, and there is nothing I can do about it," I flatly stated.

Within minutes more sounds emitted from the back. Not really wanting to know, Graham asked, "What's she doing now?"

I couldn't think of a way to soften the blow so in a matter-of-fact voice I replied "She's having a shit."

Graham was furious, "You can clean this van out and disinfect it before I take it back to work." I would have agreed to anything if it

Life on the Funny Farm

would pacify him. Susie decided she would change her position and before I could stop her she turned round pressing her rear end into Graham's neck.

"Get that goats head out of my neck," demanded Graham.

"It's not her head it's her behind," I tersely replied.

"If that goat does anything down my neck you and I are finished." I knew by the tone of his voice he wasn't joking! At last we reached the farm. I had held the lead so tightly the blood supply to my fingers had stopped. Susie leapt out of the van and immediately began to nibble the grass verge none the worse for her adventure. The same could not be said about Graham; he was still angry and when he saw the devastation in the back of the van his mood became murderous! My nerves were in complete tatters but I settled Susie in the stable and set to work cleaning the van. After such a fraught afternoon it would have been pleasant to sit down and relax but it was not to be, it was time for Susie to be milked.

Graham and I went to the stable. We took with us bucket, and cloths, I was ready with my marching tune; every verse of Onward Christian Soldiers was indelibly etched in my brain. Susie was patience personified as the milk dribbled slowly from her teats, my hands ached from the effort, the blood supply had only just returned to my fingers. Graham watched the painfully slow progress, "Here let me have a go, it can't be that difficult," he said confidently. Graham had no more success than I, but gradually, the bucket began to fill with milk. Susie became restless, after years of being milked by competent people she had inherited a couple of idiots. It was all too much for her, with one swift move of the hind leg our bucket of milk was spilt all over the stable floor. There was milk everywhere but not a drop to drink, at least not for us, Susie with great relish drank it from the floor. The saying 'crying over spilt milk' took on a whole new meaning for me, that day. Graham and I returned to the house, each blaming the other for the mishap. We spent yet another evening in a frosty silence both contemplating that morning milking would come all too soon!

Morning dawned and armed with my milking paraphernalia, I prepared to do battle with Susie and become the local answer to Heidi! My fingers had returned to normal. The practice with the rubber gloves paid off and the milking was slow but the whole process was

Chapter 9 – The Art of Kiddology

accomplished much quicker. I strained the milk and left it in the kitchen sink surrounded by cold water so it would cool. Half an hour later I returned ready to have a cup of tea with our own milk. I couldn't believe the evidence of my own eyes, my jug of milk was surrounded by the breakfast pots soaking ready for washing up. There was no alternative but to pour the contaminated milk down the drain!

It was at this moment Graham walked into the kitchen. I could not contain my anger "Fancy putting the pots in with the milk, I've poured it away. It was ruined. What possessed you to do such a thing?"

Angrily, Graham said, "I didn't ruin the milk, I realised at the last minute the milk was cooling so I didn't add any warm water or detergent. There was no need to throw it away."

I would not be pacified, "You should have removed the dishes when you realised your mistake. What else was I to think?"

Graham did not answer but the loud slam of the kitchen door reverberating around the house as he left said it all. The goat was fast becoming grounds for divorce! That evening I milked Susie without incident. The milk was cooled and strained, and I made our first cup of tea with our own milk. It did not take me long to increase my milking speed and soon there was a froth on top of the milk in the bucket. At last, I was able to say I could milk a goat. Graham returned the van to work the following morning. Some days later he told me the workforce had complained about a strange odour which had permeated the van. Graham did not enlighten them as to its cause!

Chapter 10
Peggy Joins the Team

As the height of the holiday season approached I found my days crammed with caring for our feline guests, and attending to the needs of my own animal and human family. Doris continued to do sterling work in the house but the time had come to employ someone to help with the animals. Another ad in the local Post Office again resulted in an immediate response. An eighteen-year-old local lass called Peggy came along for interview. She was a tall, well-built girl with long, blonde hair. She was quietly spoken and shared my passion for animals. During the interview I learnt that due to her contracting measles as a baby she suffered from impaired hearing. She coped extremely well with her disability but was unaware of the telephone or doorbell ringing. I quickly learnt to always face her when I spoke to her so she was able to lip-read. Customers never complained when she was slow to answer as they were aware of her sympathetic handling of their beloved pets. Peggy had just arrived for her first day of work when the doorbell rang. An agitated driver stood at the door, he had run over one of my hens. The hen had fluttered into the ditch. He took us to the place where he had last seen the hen. The little white hen lay at the bottom of the ditch. I climbed down and gently cradled the broken body; the impact had been too great for the fragile frame. Peggy stood on the bank and I passed her the lifeless bird. As I clambered out of the ditch I noticed an ashen pallor spread across Peggy's face. I took the bird from her. Concerned, I asked if she felt ill?

Chapter 10 – Peggy Joins the Team

In a trembling voice she said, "I'm sorry but I can't bear touching anything that is dead." After such a traumatic start to a new job weaker souls would have thrown in the towel but Peggy was made of sterner stuff, although in all the years she worked for me she always found handling dead animals difficult.

The farm was now a hive of activity, a vacancy arose in the stables. Within days, a lady arrived to ask if we would stable her horse. The horse called Bo was a Palomino. This has always been one of my favourite colours since watching the films of Roy Rogers and Trigger. Bo was a pleasant-natured horse, well-behaved, he was a good addition to the yard. His owner doted upon him, he wanted for nothing. The heady days of summer were drawing to a close. My trusty agricultural contractor, Bert, arrived to make hay in the last of the sunshine. The fields yielded six hundred bales which had to be safely stored in the barn. I enlisted the help of all the horse owners to move and stack the bales. At the end of our labours, we sat on the lawn in the fading sun, sharing a harvest supper. The fodder for the winter was safely stored. The days began to shorten; the trees shed their leaves as autumn descended. Bert and his helper, Steve, began work on the fields preparing them for the winter months. There was much that needed to be done. We erected post and rail fencing which entailed hiring Bert for the week. As usual, he gave me no idea as to the cost and frequently disappeared to collect the children from school. His eldest child was a girl aged eight, he had two six-year-old sons who were only born ten months apart. There was also another son who was still a toddler. One day whilst Bert was working, his wife paid him a visit. This was the first time I had met her. She was very tall, well-built with a long dark mane of hair. Her name was Kathleen. She stood talking to Bert with the toddler balanced on her hip, there was no mistaking she was expecting another child. Her reason for visiting was to inform Bert the spare part for the tractor had arrived and she had repaired it. I soon learnt that Kathleen maintained all the vehicles and thought nothing of working under a tractor even when the birth of her child was imminent. Nor was it a surprise to see Kathleen lifting bales onto the trailer in the last weeks of her pregnancy. Bert, on the other hand, was quite happy to ferry the children about and shop for their clothes. Over the years we exchanged many recipes as he was the head chef.

Life on the Funny Farm

One afternoon when Bert had gone to meet his children from school, Steve engaged me in conversation.

"You know you're very lucky that Bert will work for you. Bert can be a funny beggar at times. I've seen him walk off a job many times because he can't get on with the folk."

I was surprised as Bert seemed a genial fellow but I said, "I'm glad he finds me all right. I'd be lost without his expertise."

Steve hesitated, wondering how much he should disclose about his boss to someone he hardly knew, "He's a big man in every way. Did you know about the fire?"

I had a vague recollection, "I do remember hearing about a local farmhouse being rebuilt after a fire."

Steve began to tell me all about it, "I'd finished the day's work and left Bert to go home. I hadn't been in long when I heard sirens. We live in a block of flats so I looked out of the window to see what the commotion was. I shall never forget the moment when I saw the sky aglow from the flames coming from Bert's farm. I rushed straight back to the farm to see if I could help. I thought it would be one of the barns but when I arrived, I saw the house was an inferno. The fire engines and ambulances were there and I could see Kathleen and some of the children dishevelled and blackened with smoke. I looked for Bert but there was no sign of him. I tried to find out what was going on but it was chaotic. They brought out someone from the blazing house and placed them on a stretcher. I went and looked. At first, I did not recognise the blackened face but eventually I realised it was Bert. When I saw him like that I thought he was dead. They took him to the hospital he had inhaled a lot of smoke and had sustained burns. You see, he kept going back into the house to save the children. He got them all out except for his youngest son. He perished in the fire."

I listened with horror as the tragedy unfolded. My admiration for Bert soared; he was a courageous man who bore his tragedy with dignity. It was a number of months before Bert told me about the death of his son. I knew then Bert and his family had accepted me as a friend.

As Bert was putting the finishing touches to the fencing he came to see me.

Chapter 10 – Peggy Joins the Team

"Anna, I've been thinking, you know what you could do?"

I wondered what was coming. Bert tipped his cap forward, scratched his head and his familiar thoughtful expression spread across his face. "You have the ideal place to keep a pig."

"I don't know anything about pigs," I quickly replied.

Confidently, Bert said, "You'll soon learn. You will like pigs they are wonderful creatures. Get yourself a book. I know a number of pig keepers. We can soon find you one."

If Bert thought it a good idea, I had complete faith in his judgement but there was a little matter that gave me some concern, "You're forgetting one thing. I don't think Graham is going to be too keen on the idea of a pig, he has only just gotten used to the goats."

Bert shrugged, "I'm sure you can get round him, tell him how marvellous home grown pork tastes."

I did not share Bert's confidence, but when Graham returned from work and had settled down in his chair I brought the subject up.

"Bert has finished the fencing today. We got into conversation; he thinks we ought to have a pig." I waited for a response.

"I think we've got quite enough animals already. Bert can keep his ideas to himself."

I could tell by Graham's voice there was no point pursuing the matter. However, I would not give up. I had a plan of action in mind!

Chapter 11
A Champion is Born

The year had sped by, Joe and Lucy were now able to walk and they had begun to utter their first words. As a treat, we took the twins to visit a nearby zoo. There they saw all kinds of creatures from the confines of their twin buggy. Lucy became animated when she saw a huge Tiger pacing around the perimeter of his enclosure. Until now, the only words they had uttered which we were able to
decipher were mumma and dada. But now, at the sight of the glorious striped beast, Lucy began to point with an outstretched arm, at the same time shouting, "Bluebell!" I was amazed she was calling the Tiger the name of our young Burmese cat Bluebell. Clearly, Lucy could identify the fact that they belonged to the same species. Perhaps I had reared a cat fanatic of the future! Lucy continued to mispronounce Bluebell's name for many months to come. Christmas was fast approaching and the cattery was fully booked for the festive break. I realised that we would not be able to visit our family over Christmas as we had so many animals to look after. The solution was simple. The family would spend Christmas at the farm. This set the pattern for future years; the house would be filled with guests celebrating Yuletide. During the year I had successfully mated my cats and their kittens had all been found loving homes. Our resident cat population had continued to expand; I now had four breeding girls. The latest was a brown Burmese called Fleur. Fleur was small for the breed, she had a short tail and ears which sat upright on her head giv-

Chapter 11 – A Champion is Born

ing the impression they had been stuck on as an afterthought. She would not have won any prizes at a show but I adored her. She had a huge personality; she was a better retriever than any dog, she was very affectionate and intelligent. Fleur could open all the doors in the house. She would jump onto the handle and use the weight of her body to bring the handle down. The moment she heard it click she would jump down and paw the door ajar. Doorknobs did not present her with any difficulty; she learnt to swing her body from side to side until she heard that magical click. Electric light switches were treated to the same attentions. Many mornings I would awake to find the house bathed in electric light. Some evenings, I would settle down to read a book. My relaxation was soon spoilt by Fleur, who would flick the light switch off. Stumbling through the dark to illuminate the room, my only reward would be for Fleur to repeat the process! Fleur decided to come into call at Christmas. She managed to keep our guests awake with her caterwauling.

In the New Year Fleur visited a stud in Middlesex. All did not go well; Fleur would not let the boyfriend near her. The stud owner phoned to ask me if I had any ideas. I thought for a few moments
"Fleur loves her food, have you got any rabbit?"

She quickly replied she had a whole rabbit in her freezer.

"Simple then, feed her all of it then let the stud in with her. She will be so bloated she won't be able to escape his attentions." My prediction was correct, and once Fleur had been mated she was in love and gave no more trouble to the stud. In the future, I would repeat this successful mating and the stud owner always made sure there was whole rabbit waiting for Fleur

Two months later, Fleur produced a litter of eight kittens. Very soon it was clear that one of the kittens stood out from the rest. It was a chocolate, male kitten. He had his mother's personality but not her looks. This kitten oozed star quality. I named the litter after characters from the book Lord of The Rings. This kitten bore the name Bilbo Baggins, affectionately known as Bill. It went without saying Bill was not for sale. If he was as good as I thought, he would become my stud cat in the future. As soon as he was old enough, Bill was shown and I was not disappointed. The judges agreed with me, he was a class act. Bill loved the shows but in the afternoon he would become bored and chew his blanket. It is not uncommon for some breeds to eat wool-like materials, particularly Siamese and Burmese. After each show I would have to buy another blanket. It was becoming a costly business. At home, Bill's favourite treat was a raw marrowbone. I decided to take one to the shows with me and place it in his pen after judging. This treat worked on Bill, he gnawed on his bone and never chewed a blanket again. It also caused a great stir amongst the judges, exhibitors and visitors to the show. Bill would hurl the bone around the pen entertaining the onlookers with his strength. He became a celebrity and people would scan the rows of pens searching for the cat with the bone!

I didn't realise how his fame had spread until I was out shopping one day at the local parade of shops. As I was entering a shop, I heard a voice, "Excuse me, aren't you Bilbo Baggins' mum?" I turned around and saw a small woman about my age, sporting a crash helmet and huge padded jacket. I had never before been identified in this way. Curious, I replied "Yes, how do you know about Bill?"

"My name is Meg, I breed Birmans and Chinchillas. I've seen him at the shows with his bone." I didn't know it then but Meg and I were to become firm friends. We not only had cats in common but also, Meg was the daughter of a local farmer. I would soon have another source of knowledge for my farming enterprise. We arranged to meet and have coffee together. Right from the start I knew we were kindred spirits. Meg was my kind of person; she had no airs or graces, she was plain speaking and what you see is what you get. Meg soon conveyed her considerable knowledge of animals. As she lived close by, and did not have any means of transport other than her scooter, it was only natural that we should start to travel to shows together. Over the years we shared laughter and tears but come what may we were always there for each other.

Chapter 12
Pork is on the Menu

I had not given up the idea of acquiring a pig. Over the past weeks, I had embarked on a strategy designed to win Graham over. Graham was very fond of his food, he appreciated quality meals. I had purchased numerous cheap, mass-produced joints of pork and all had one thing in common, they lacked flavour. Graham had eaten them all without comment until one evening, munching his way through tea, Graham stopped and looked towards me, "Ann, I'm getting tired of this pork, did you get a cheap lot because it seems to have no taste?"

My answer was well rehearsed, "The trouble is, it is very difficult to buy meat at a reasonable price that has not been mass-produced. If we produced our own meat I'm sure we would get better quality."

In a resigned voice Graham said, "This hasn't anything to do with getting a pig, has it?"

I knew my plan had at long last succeeded, "We could give it a try, and we could even have home-cured bacon."

Graham sat and deliberated a while, "Ok, go ahead but I want to get one thing straight from the beginning, any animals we rear are for meat and exactly that. If they don't go for slaughter, the whole lot can be sold."

I agreed readily, it would be a long time before any were ready to eat and I would deal with that when the time came.

When Bert next paid us a visit I told him Graham had agreed I should have a pig. Bert knew of a farmer a couple of miles away that would be willing to sell me one of his pigs. Bert arranged for me to visit. The farm was down a long drive. When I finally drew up outside the house, I could hear and see a band of farm dogs ready to spring into action. I had experienced the aggressive nature of farmyard dogs before so I sounded my horn and waited for someone to come to my aid. A tall muscular woman came out of the house. She called the dogs to heel, and beckoned me out of the car. With the dogs under control I followed her into the house. The house would not have been featured in Homes and Gardens; it was cluttered and grimy. I walked to a back room, which resembled an outhouse. In the chair sat her husband, Dennis, he was a tall, painfully thin man who looked far from well. As he stood up his shoulders were hunched but I was surprised at his strength and vigour.

Dennis spoke, "Sit down lass."

I scanned the room. The few chairs were all occupied by numerous Persian cats, but in the far corner was a cage built into the wall, from which a Barn Owl stared malevolently. I gently moved a cat to one side and perched on the edge of the chair. A big Alsatian dog came up to me and sniffed curiously at this stranger. Absentmindedly, I stroked the dog's head. Bert had warned me that Dennis did not suffer fools gladly, and as Dennis eyed me up and down I felt he was unimpressed by this slip of a woman in front of him.

"Bert tells me you want a pig, do you know anything about them?"

Nervously, I replied, "No, only what I have read in books, but I'm sure Bert will help me if I have any problems."

"You can't beat hands on experience, a book can only tell you so much."

I agreed with Dennis and said, "I'm willing to learn."

Dennis looked across the room to his wife, "Look at that dog, it's amazing." His wife nodded her head in agreement. "What's amazing?" I enquired.

Smiling, Dennis said, "I have never seen the dog you are stroking be so taken with a stranger, he usually bites them!"

I looked down at the dog and casually removed my hand. Dennis took delight in my discomfort but I had come for a pig and I wasn't going away empty handed.

Chapter 12 - Pork is on the Menu

Dennis took me outside and gave me a tour of his farm. He had a pedigree herd of Ayrshire cows of which he was justly proud. He also had a herd of Aberdeen Angus, which he reared for beef. He took me into a cattle shed and showed me a group of young calves, "If you want to produce your own meat, you could do worse than buying a couple of these," he said. I ignored the comment and we continued to make our way to the pigs. As we walked, numerous cats danced around our feet. I couldn't help but comment, "I have never been to a farm where all the cats are pedigree Persians." His eyes lit up, "Cats are my favourite animals. My wife prefers her dogs, but give me a cat any day." We chatted companionably about cats, breeding and showing when at last, we reached the pigsties. Each sty was brick-built with a walled exercise area. Like all the animal housing on the farm, it was kept in an immaculate condition – a complete opposite of where the humans dwelt. He had all types of pigs but a large pink spotted pig caught my eye. "Oh I like this one, what is it?"

Dennis saw my enthusiasm and relaxed, "That is a Gloucester Old Spot. In fact it would be a good breed for you to begin with. They are an old fashioned breed, very hardy and docile."

"Have you got any of them for sale?" I eagerly enquired.

"I haven't got any weaners but this one is a young pig. If you want her, she is yours."

I looked at the spotty pig; she was a full-grown gilt who had reached sexual maturity, Where was the sense in buying weaners when I would be able to breed my own?

"If I bought her where could I find a boar to service her?" I asked.

Happily, he replied, "I have a boar here. I could mate her for you and when I am sure she is in pig you could collect her." It was too good an opportunity to let slip so the deal was agreed. I returned home and waited patiently for my sow to join me.

Chapter 13
Bringing Home the Bacon

Graham fully expected to return home and find a pig in residence. He was surprised to find this was not so. "Didn't you sort a pig out after all?" he asked. I told him the matter was in hand.

A month passed before Dennis rang to say the pig was pregnant. He agreed to bring her as he wanted to see where she would live.

Dennis and spotty pig duly arrived. Dennis was impressed with her quarters and had no qualms about entrusting her to my care. As he was leaving he gave me a warning, "Now don't go ruining that pig, feed her properly and don't make a fool out of her. By the way she has a name, I call her Gertie." I promised I would take good care of her and not overfeed her. Within minutes, I found Gertie was a friendly pig who loved her back being scratched with the yard broom. She was happy as a pig in clover in her new surroundings.

When Graham returned home from work, I introduced him to Gertie. As he peered into the stable his face registered disbelief, "You have done it again, that's a fully grown pig. I thought you were getting a weaner." I noticed the ominous tone in his voice.

"We shall have weaners soon enough she is pregnant."

Graham shouted "What! How many piglets do they have?"

I hesitated before I replied, "Well they can have quite a few."

"What do you mean by quite a few?" Graham demanded to know.

Chapter 12 - Pork is on the Menu

Very quickly, I said, "It's not unusual for them to have a dozen." I began to realise another evening of frosty silence was stretching before me.

Angrily, Graham said, "Let me tell you now, don't think you are dragging me out here in the middle of the night because she has got problems in labour."

Confidently I said, "If there is a problem I'm sure Bert would help."

"I shall have words with Bert when I next see him. He gave you the idea. I hold him responsible." If the past was anything to go by, I knew Graham would eventually calm down. But until then, Gertie had better stay out of his way!

Chapter 14
Basil the Billy Goat

A pig's pregnancy lasts for five months so I would have to be patient and wait for my first piglets to be born. As a teacher, my year had been divided in to terms. But now I worked with the seasons. Summer was once again approaching. My days were extremely long, beginning at five thirty in the morning and ending when the light faded. I was kept busy looking after all the animals, which continued to expand in numbers. Joe and Lucy attended nursery school each morning which meant I met other mothers in the village. I was fortunate to have made many friends.

Meg was a frequent visitor; she lived alone and often called in to share a coffee and a chat. One morning she brought the gift of a Muscovy duck, it was a large grey and white bird. Joe and Lucy thought she was wonderful and named her Gemima. She soon became a firm favourite with them. As summer arrived, Gemima spent many happy hours playing with them in the paddling pool! Most children have to make do with a plastic duck in the bath but mine had the real thing!

Life on the farm had fallen into a routine. The cattery was a success, our customer base was growing steadily, and, financially, we were more secure. At last, we could relax. This air of confidence had spread to the goats. Angie was now an adult, for the uninitiated goat can only produce milk if periodically it produces a kid. We had enjoyed our own milk so it was necessary to mate Angie, if our supply was to continue. Susie was over ten years old when she came to live with us.

Chapter 14 – Basil the Billy Goat

I decided not to mate her again; she had done her bit and could retire. As the warmth of summer surrounded us Angie came into season, she let us know by her persistent bleating and vigorous wagging tail. I had done my research and found a Billy goat a few miles away. I enlisted the help of Peggy, and we parcelled Angie into the rear of my estate car and set off on our journey. The journey was uneventful; we arrived relaxed with no sense of foreboding. I went to the house and rang the doorbell. Eventually, the door opened. An elderly lady stood in the doorway.

"Hello," I said, "I've brought my nanny goat as we arranged to be served by your billy."

The lady appeared agitated as she spoke, "The girl who helps me is not here today and I am partially blind. I'm afraid I won't be of much use, but you can take your goat down to the bottom paddock yourself. Basil is there, he's a very elderly goat you won't have any problems."

My confidence ebbed away, the only thing I knew about mating goats I had gleaned from books and from past experience. Books don't tell you everything! However, I decided to go ahead. I walked back to Peggy who was holding Angie on her lead.

In a matter-of-fact voice, I said, "There's been a slight hitch. There is no one to help us. We will have to take Angie down ourselves."

Peggy's face suddenly took on the appearance of a frightened rabbit, "What are we going to do?" she asked.

With all the confidence I could muster I said, "Simple, you can hold Angie and I will take charge of Basil. He is very elderly so he shouldn't be too difficult."

We walked down towards the paddock and in the distance I caught my first sight of Basil. He was in the far corner of the field grazing happily. As we approached, he raised his head and curled his top lip up to savour the scent of a nanny in season. Suddenly his whole demeanour changed, he began to paw the ground like a miniature bull, at the same time emitting what sounded like a deep-throated roar. By now, we had reached the gate. There was no going back. Peggy assessed the situation and before I knew what was happening she thrust Angie's lead in to my hand and beat a hasty retreat to the safety of a nearby hedge. Basil was now in full gallop, Angie was unconcerned but my life flashed before me as Basil honed in on his target! His aim was as deadly as an exact missile. At full speed he launched himself on to Angie's back. The impact sent me sprawling to the ground. Within minutes his mission was accomplished. I picked myself up, and with Angie in tow hobbled out of the paddock. Peggy ran to meet me, in a relieved voice she said, "You were brave."

Wearily, I replied, "I had no choice, I just hope she is pregnant, I couldn't go through that again if you paid me!"

The journey home was uneventful as unlike Susie, Angie enjoyed motorised travel. However, for the entire trip home we travelled with all the windows wound down fully as the odour of Billy goat is one of the most overpowering and offensive smells you could wish to experience. When we returned, Peggy took Angie to her stable, and I rushed indoors for a much needed bath. I heard Doris shout, "Where have you been?"

"You don't want to know" was my quick reply. Doris appeared at my side, a genuine look of horror filled her eyes, "You're covered in mud. What have you been doing, has there been an accident? What's that dreadful smell?"

I told Doris about our trip to see Basil and how it had resulted in me sprawled across the ground. Doris busied herself by making a cup of tea, the cure for all ills.

Chapter 15
Porcine Pranks

That summer it appeared that all the animals had put reproduction at the top of their agenda. My cats regularly produced kittens and I was fortunate to find them all doting slaves to pander to their every whim for the rest of their lives. Gertie was now heavily pregnant. During the day, she had her own garden where she spent hours excavating with her powerful snout. She had ploughed the piece of waste ground expertly, and on warm summer days loved to roll in the damp earth. Gertie was blessed with a wonderful nature; she loved human company, had a passion for food, her favourite being cheese and onion crisps. If given the choice, she would always select that flavour. Gertie would stop whatever she was doing the moment she heard the rattle of a crisp packet and run to investigate. This proved very useful on the occasion she escaped from her garden. Gertie decided to explore the farm. She managed to coincide her amble down the drive with a customer arriving with his cat. I had already realised Gertie was loose and had fetched her favourite crisps but before I could intervene the customer had entered the farm. The gentleman had his two cats in a carrier. As he walked in, he saw a large pig walking with a purposeful air towards him. He did no more than drop the carrier and vault over the farm gate! Gertie was unconcerned, she went towards the carrier and sniffed at it curiously, hoping it contained an edible treat. Her disappointment soon vanished when she heard the familiar sound of a crisp packet being opened. Obediently, she followed me back to her garden. I tried to reassure the customer that Gertie was harmless but I do not think he believed me. That was the last time I boarded his cats, the thought of meeting a run away pig again was obviously too much for him! Fortunately, most of my customers enjoy seeing the different animals and over the years have gotten to know many of them well.

Angie was also pregnant. Not to be outdone, one of the hens had become broody and was sitting on a clutch of eggs. A broody hen is a formidable sight as they puff out their feathers to give the impression of a much larger bird; without hesitation they will peck viciously at anything, which comes near the nest. Three weeks later the chicks began to hatch. In the first few days, I was overjoyed to catch a glimpse of the chicks as they peeked out at the world from the safety of their mother's wing. Rose and Fred were visiting and I asked Rose if she would like to see the young chicks. Rose was keen to see them so we went to the pen. We were lucky the chicks were busy pecking their chick feed. Rose watched in amazement and said, "Isn't it wonderful they are feeding themselves so soon? You think they would get enough from their mother's milk."

I looked at her face and realised she was being serious, it was time to enlighten her, "Birds don't produce milk for their young, only mammals do that."

Stunned by her lesson in biology she replied, "Well, I never knew that." It was then I realised how entrenched she was in city life. For all her years she had missed out on so much, no wonder she found our life style hard to understand.

Gertie was showing signs that the birth of her piglets was imminent. She had begun to make a nest in her straw bed and each day she became increasingly restless. Bert had visited regularly to see how she was progressing; he stood, tipping his cap forward, scratching his head and delivered his pearls of wisdom, "It won't be long now, Anna. We will rig up a bar in the corner as some sows manage to roll on the piglets and kill them. That will give the piglets an escape route."

I looked at Gertie and said, "I don't think she would harm them, she's a good natured pig."

Bert shook his head. He warned me, "Anna, this isn't one of your cats having kittens. Pigs can be mean. She won't think twice about biting you if you interfere with her youngsters. I've seen experienced

Chapter 15 – Porcine Pranks

farmers attacked by their sows; you must be careful." I knew Bert well enough to know that he was being serious and was concerned for my safety. I had every intention of heeding his warning. As things turned out, Bert need not have worried. Gertie went into labour early that evening and I sat in the stable talking to her. She gave birth effortlessly to nine piglets that were all healthy, and immediately proved they had voracious appetites as they fought for control of the teats. Gertie was quite content to let me share in the miracle of nature and made no objection when I handled the tiny, smooth pink bundles. She was an excellent mother, who always seemed to know instinctively where her piglets lay and never hurt one of them. My first litter of piglets were safely into the world and for me it had been completely stress-free.

Chapter 16
Gertie Gets Annoyed

As the piglets grew Gertie was pleased to show them to everyone who visited, not once showing any aggression. I put to the back of my mind Bert's warning;it may apply to some pigs but not to my Gertie! We moved mother and the piglets to a large building by the house which had its own paddock so they could play outside during the day. Some of the piglets were boars so I arranged for the vet to castrate them. At the same time they would have the tips of their teeth cut off as they have very sharp teeth and these rip the flesh of the sow mercilessly as they suckle. Some months earlier my vet had employed two new vets, a husband and wife team. The husband, a Scot called Angus, was a tall, powerfully built Rugby enthusiast, his wife was equally tall, with long fair hair, who came from New Zealand her name was Shona. It was decided that Shona should attend to the piglets.

One afternoon she arrived to carry out her veterinary skills, I took her to meet the porcine family. Gertie was happy to show off her brood and we gathered the piglets together in the building, we left Gertie outside in the paddock. I quickly caught a piglet and handed it to Shona. The moment she opened its mouth, an ear splitting squeal echoed around the building. Pigs when they are upset have a unique range of vocalisations, and on hearing their littermate squeal, all nine of them began to scream at the top of their voices. The only sound that could compete with them was the loud snorting of their irate mother, accompanied by heavy thuds as Gertie, head down like a Rhino in full charge, butted the stable door. The door shook from

Chapter 15 – Porcine Pranks

the impact, the bolts rattling each time the door was assaulted. I remembered Bert's warning and it was no exaggeration I was gripped by fear.

Shona was no longer the cool professional, shouting above the din she said, "We must get these piglets back to the mother as soon as I have treated them." That was easier said than done. To open the door would have been a suicidal act, I scanned the building for inspiration and saw an old door lying on the floor. With my mind working overtime I said, "If we open the top part of the door and then lift this old door outside we could use it as a slide. As we finish each piglet we can slide it down to Gertie." Shona could not think of anything better, so we rigged up the apparatus. The piglets squealed as they slid to the bottom, they then ran to their mother but nothing would pacify her. At last, all the piglets were outside with their mother, but her mood had not altered. Shona and I were trapped in the building. Gertie repeatedly stormed the door. Time passed by, and as we hoped, Gertie's temper mellowed. Eventually, she walked to the far end of the paddock. Shona said, "This is our chance, we will have to make a run for it..If we dash to the fence and climb over, it can't be more than twelve feet away. She might not even notice us." I didn't share Shona's optimism, but there was nothing else we could do. Shona went first, her long legs covering the ground effortlessly. She vaulted over the fence in the style of a first class athlete. My turn came. With my short legs, I produced a burst of speed that I didn't know I was capable of, but Gertie caught sight of my attempted escape and she had a score to settle. Her snout was only inches away from me as I reached the fence. Shona grabbed my shoulders and pulled me to safety. Gertie hurled herself at my retreating back. It took Gertie two days to forgive me, and a whole box of cheese and onion crisps. From that time on when piglets needed treatment Gertie was safely locked away!

Chapter 17
A Difficult Birth

I had gained confidence from the piglet's easy delivery, and I was looking forward with keen anticipation to the delivery of Angie's kid. One bright sunny morning Angie decided her time to give birth had arrived. Peggy and I kept a careful watch as the labour progressed. Everything was going according to plan, so well that I wondered if Angie had studied the books, and then suddenly Angie digressed from the script! She became agitated and as she strained with the contractions her bleating became louder and more pained, there was no doubt she was in trouble. I told Peggy, " Stay with her while I phone the vet." I rushed indoors sure I would soon have expert help. My vet Neville, was operating and the others were all out on visits it would be some time before anyone could arrive. I was panic struck but my vet calmly spoke to me. "You can help the goat yourself, have you got a mobile phone?" I replied in the affirmative.

"Scrub down your hands and arms with disinfectant, take your mobile with you and I will talk you through the delivery." His matter-of fact-tone did nothing to quell my fears. I returned to the stable with buckets of warm water, mobile phone and my goat keeper's handbook. Peggy greeted my return with relief, "I'm glad you are back, she is getting in a real state. When will the vet be here?"

Quickly I replied, "He can't come at the moment, he's operating, I'm going to speak to him over the phone and he will tell me what to do."

Angie was beside herself, she was bearing down trying to produce a kid, which stubbornly refused to budge. I rang my vet and explained

Chapter 15 – Porcine Pranks

the situation. Neville asked if I could see the kid. I replied that I thought I could see a foot. "This is what you must do," Neville said, "Clearly, it is a problem presentation. Look in your book and familiarise yourself with the different presentations, then put your hands inside the goat and see if you can discover which way the kid is lying." With trembling hands I passed the phone to Peggy and studied the book. Tentatively I slid my hands inside Angie, I looked at Peggy and said, "I can't do this, I'll hurt her." Peggy supportively said, "She isn't bleating as much now so you can't be doing any damage, keep going." With those words of encouragement my hands explored the body of the kid. Amazingly, I found the problem; the legs instead of being outstretched were tucked up under the chest. I told Peggy, and she relayed the message to Neville. Neville told me how to straighten the legs and within minutes a huge contraction from Angie propelled the kid on to the stable floor.

Relief surged through my body, the kid was alive and Angie immediately began to lick the wet bedraggled Billy kid. I could understand the job satisfaction experienced by doctors and midwives when a new life enters the world with their help. My euphoria did not last long; Angie began to contract again. This time there wasn't a problem, a nanny kid slipped out with no help from me. Over the years I have intervened at many births but the first time was an unbelievable experience; I was filled with wonder at the complexity of nature.

Summer was drawing to a close. The piglets were growing rapidly, the kids gambolled around the farm, and the chicks strutted independently around the farm. There was plenty of work to do and many mouths to feed. The hay had been cut and was safely stored in the barn ready for another winter. Graham had been engrossed in his work over the summer months and had left the running of the farm to me. He didn't even comment on the expanding number of livestock, which I found disconcerting. Graham had something on his mind, soon all would be revealed.

Chapter 18
Building Plans

It soon became abundantly clear what Graham had been planning. Graham rang from work one day, and said, "Anne when I come home tonight there is something we must discuss."

That evening we settled down to talk. Graham began, "Anne when we moved into the farm we both agreed that as soon as possible we would extend the bungalow, I think that time has come." I knew the plans he had in mind, I also knew it would be a tremendous upheaval and I had put the idea to the back of my mind, but Graham was determined to enlarge our home. Reluctantly, I said, "You do realise how difficult it will make our lives; it isn't just an extra room you are talking about, but two bedrooms, a bathroom, kitchen, utility not to mention a double garage."

Graham was not to be deterred, "The children are growing up, we will need the extra space. I know an architect and he will draw the plans up for us. We shall have to find a builder. Ask Meg who renovated her cottage. I have always thought they did a wonderful job turning that 'one up one down' into such a lovely house." When Graham set his mind to something there was no way to dissuade him. I agreed the time had come to turn the bungalow into something quite different, but not before I made two requests.

"Graham if we are going ahead with the building I want a walk in pantry, and our existing bedroom I want to turn into a maternity suite for my cats."

Chapter 18 – Building Plans

Graham readily agreed and within weeks the plans were devised. To enable us to have the extra rooms a staircase would have to be fitted, so the house would no longer be a bungalow. The plans were submitted to the local council and we waited for them to accept them in due course. It was not to be; they did not like the plans and said, 'It was not in keeping with the area'. The architect pleaded our case, finally the council agreed to have a meeting of the Planning Committee on site. The day arrived when the committee trooped on to the farm; it was a sunny day, and I sat on the lawn with the children. When they entered the gate I strolled over and followed them onto the lawn. The leader of the committee looked towards the back of the group and shouted, "This is a private meeting, no public are allowed."

Beside me was a young woman; I thought she must be a customer who had inadvertently joined the group. Before I could say anything to her, the man shouted again, "It's you I'm talking to! Go away while we discuss the application."

It was then I realised it was me he was addressing, not the young woman! I was furious but I could not afford to alienate the council if we wanted our extension. I rejoined the children and watched as they deliberated over the plans. I wasn't the only observer; sitting quietly under the tree were the geese, they raised their long elegant necks and slowly stood up. The Planning Committee may have ideas of grandeur, but as far as my geese were concerned they were interlopers and must be dealt with. I knew what was coming, and a smile of smug satisfaction crossed my face; it was like lambs to the slaughter. The geese homed in on their quarry, necks outstretched, wings ominously flapping. At first some of the councillors waved their arms at the birds making shooing noises. But this only made the geese more determined, as they raised their bodies to full height and ran into the group of people. People scattered in all directions all with one aim, to reach the safety of the gate. The geese were by now well into their stride, nipping trouser legs and grabbing beakfulls of ladies skirts. The precious plans and briefcases were being deployed as shields but the attack was relentless.

The leader bellowed to me, " Don't just sit there do something!"

Sweetly I replied, " Sorry, it is a private meeting. I can't attend."

Life on the Funny Farm

Finally the group in disarray stood outside the gate gathering their wits. The geese did a slow lap of honour around the lawn; they had once again repelled all boarders. Whether it was the thought of another site visit I shall never know, but there were no further objections to our plans. The extension could go ahead with the council's blessing!

Chapter 19
The Plans are Put into Action

We approached a number of builders and decided to entrust Meg's builder with the work. The builder named Kevin was a big burly man who spent his weekends playing Rugby. After studying the plans he told us he would begin work in June and it should all be finished by October. This meant it would coincide with the holiday season, my busiest time of the year, but there was nothing I could do about it. Kevin told me that for the first couple of months there would be no disruption to the main body of the house, but eventually we would have to move out while they altered the existing building. We could not leave the farm so Graham began to search for a mobile home, which we could site on the lawn.

Kevin was as good as his word; at the beginning of June he arrived with his work force. They settled in for the long hard graft. During the months ahead a number of various craftsmen would join the team to concentrate on their own specialised area, but Gerry and John would remain on site throughout the building process. Gerry in his early twenties was tall, blonde, and forever cheerful, singing the latest hit tunes at the top of his voice; John on the other hand, was in his fifties a quiet man who took great pride in his brick laying. As soon as they arrived the first job they undertook was to demolish the ramshackle conservatory, it did not take much brute force to reduce it to a pile of rubble. As I surveyed the devastation outside my back door I knew there was no going back, my home had become a building site!

Life on the Funny Farm

Throughout the summer we managed to operate the cattery. The customers watched the building progress with interest. Whilst the builders were in residence I had decided not to let any of my cats have kittens but I planned to have a litter born at the end of October when the house was finished. The farm animals would not be affected by the renovations, their lives would continue as normal. However, from the outset I found it very disruptive, life was not going to be normal for us. Not only was life much more difficult, I had the added worry of Joe and Lucy. The twins were nearly five years old and keen to help the builders. They did not appreciate the dangers and I was constantly watchful being the typical mother hen. My cheerful disposition began to wane and I began to experience a feeling of defeat.

Doris found cleaning difficult as everything was permanently covered in a layer of brick dust but she valiantly battled through. I wondered if she could work an extra morning. I wasn't very hopeful, I knew she had another job, but I decided to ask anyway. Her reply was immediate. "Ooh, I'd be only too happy, I gave up my other job a few weeks ago. It was boring working there!"

I was glad someone found life on the farm entertaining! My mother-in-law, Rose, was aware I was struggling to cope with the upheaval and suggested that Fred and I visit The Royal Show for a day. My father had taken me to many agricultural shows as a child and I had enjoyed them immensely. I jumped at the chance for a day out away from the building chaos. One Wednesday morning Fred and I set off for the Royal, it is a huge show which is spread over many acres. There are numerous car parks, and entrances. Fred was keen to explore all the attractions but I was careful to note where we had parked and at which gate we gained entry. The last thing we needed was not to be able to find the car at the end of the day. Once inside the show ground we went our separate ways, agreeing to meet up for lunch. I went straight to the livestock section – heaven on earth for someone like me. Every breed of pig, goat and sheep was represented. I visited the cattle sheds where the tiny Dexters were dwarfed by the gigantic Charolais, and doe-eyed Jerseys looked kindly on the visitors. As I progressed down the rows of cattle my attention suddenly focused on a red shaggy cow with enormous handle bar horns. At her side was a brown Teddy bear of a calf. I knew they were Highland cattle but I

Chapter 19 – The Plans are put into Action

had never been so close to one before. I chatted to the breeders and found out a little about their needs and characteristics. If I was ever going to have cattle, these were the breed for me!

The time sped by and as we had arranged, I met Fred for lunch. The afternoon raced by and all too soon it was time to leave. Fred and I were tired. Between us we had walked miles. Fred was keen to get home. I asked, "Do you know which gate we came in?"

Confidently, he replied, " Yes, follow me."

We set off, I knew we needed gate number four. It did not take me long to realise that Fred was taking us round the show ground in ever decreasing circles, we were getting no nearer the exit. I began to think I was in the Hampton Court maze so I decided to take charge. Over each entrance was a huge inflated balloon with the gate number displayed. As we neared the balloon Fred announced, "We are going in the wrong direction again."

I was amazed that Fred could read the number on the balloon at such a distance. With admiration, I said, "You have got good eyesight. I can't read the number on the balloon."

Fred looked puzzled and asked, "What number?"

It was my turn to be puzzled. I explained, "Each balloon has a gate number on it, what did you think?"

Embarrassed, Fred said, "I didn't realise there was a balloon at each gate. I thought there was only one where we came in, so every time I saw a balloon I headed towards it. I did begin to wonder why it kept changing position."

We had been aimlessly wandering around for half an hour but finally we reached our gate and wearily wended our way to the car. I have never let Fred forget his balloon blunder!

My trip to The Royal Show was a real tonic. I returned home eager to tell Graham about all the different animals I'd seen.

The spring in my step had returned, Graham asked about the show. I eagerly told him, "You should have come. There are so many breeds of pigs and goats, I even saw the cattle. There were some Highland cattle and I got talking to the breeders. I'm sure they would fit in just right on the farm." Graham butted in, "Oh my God! Stop there, I know where this is going – and we aren't!" I did not bother to reply. Graham had said the same about pigs but I didn't think I should bring that to his attention. My mind was set.

Chapter 20
New Foundations

The building work was progressing slowly but surely. After weeks of hard work the foundations were laid and numerous ready mixed concrete lorries began to arrive. Gerry and John spent one Friday laying the concrete and painstakingly smoothing the surface. I was concerned the animals may spoil their work and volunteered to keep the birds confined to their houses, but Gerry said there was no need. The odd footprint here and there would not matter, as it was not the final finish. By five o' clock the men had finished their task and they packed away the tools and departed for the weekend. I busied myself preparing all the animal meals; whilst I worked I heard strange noises outside the back door. I stopped working and went to investigate. The geese were in the centre of the newly laid concrete, clearly having a ball! They had paddled over the whole area and for good measure sat down and rolled in the mixture, the smooth surface now resembled an angry sea of concrete waves. I quickly rounded them up but not before they had managed to cause more damage. I dreaded the return of the builders on Monday morning, what ever would they say?

The weekend passed by uneventfully but the concrete had now completely dried out resembling the undulating surface of the moon. On Monday morning Kevin arrived with his workforce. My courage had deserted me and I hid in the bedroom, but I could not fail to hear their reaction. In a loud voice Kevin yelled, "What the bloody

Chapter 20 - New Foundations

hell has been going on?" Gerry and John rushed to the scene. After a moment of stunned silence Gerry said, "It wasn't like that when we left, it was perfectly smooth." Kevin snapped, "Well it's not smooth now is it? Where's Ann? She must know what's happened." I heard them shouting my name. I could not hide for ever; I would have to go and face the music. I explained the geese were the culprits and from now on I would keep them confined. Kevin was far from pleased but he managed to keep his temper and said, "It's too late now, they must have been bathing in the stuff." He had no idea how right he was! Some years later, I met Kevin by chance, and asked how his business was faring. Kevin told me that presently they were working on a job for a lady who had a dog. Gerry had built a neat concrete step and before it had set the dog had walked across it leaving paw prints.

The lady was very apologetic but Gerry had brushed her worries aside and said, "This is nothing, one place we worked at was a farm where a flock of geese had a party in my concrete."

Kevin said, "I knew exactly where he was talking about!"

The building work was progressing but life on the farm still had to go on. My father-in-law, Fred, came to me one day with a suggestion. "Ann, you know we always give each of our workers a turkey at Christmas. How would you like to supply the firm with the birds this year?" I knew nothing about turkeys but I told Fred I would give the matter some thought. I decided to consult the oracle, and ask Bert for advice.

Bert pondered over the idea, he tipped his cap forward and scratched his head, "I think it is a good idea Anna. It will bring in a tidy sum of money just in time for Christmas. That big shelter in the field would be ideal for keeping Turkeys. How many are you planning to rear?"

I replied, "I think fifty would be enough, but how will I get them killed and dressed?" Bert confidently said, "There are lots of people around here who will sort out the killing and plucking, and I know someone who can supply you with some poults."

Mystified I asked, "What are poults?"

Bert smiled, "That is what we call young turkeys. I must warn you it is highly unlikely you will rear all the birds you buy, the mortality rate can be quite high." I still thought fifty birds would be enough so

Life on the Funny Farm

Bert organised the purchase and we set about preparing the shelter. Before long the poults arrived. They were white birds, a mixture of stags and hens. As they grew it became clear which were stags. They became much larger and when they became excited their pink heads turned a deep shade of purple. I tended to their every need but they lacked personality, and I found it was too much like real commercial farming. I was certain these would be the first and last turkeys I would rear.

Chapter 21
Farewell to Susie

Late summer approached and I became worried about Susie, our goat. Lately, she had become reluctant to leave her stable. She no longer sought the company of Angie and the kids, preferring to lie on her bed most of the day. I decided to ask the vet to call.

Neville arrived and gave her a thorough examination. Sadly, he said, "She hasn't got any disease. The problem is Anno Domini. Her joints are arthritic and she is in some discomfort."

"Are you telling me there is nothing you can do?" I asked.

"I'm sorry, Ann, but there is no cure for old age. If she was my goat I would end her misery." Neville stood waiting for my decision. There really was no choice. Susie did not deserve to spend the remainder of her life in pain.

I said, "If you think it is for the best then you had better put her to sleep, but before you do I just want to give her a treat." I ran down to the house and poured some white wine into a wineglass, I returned to Neville and Susie.

Neville was puzzled, "Who's the drink for?"

I told him, "It's for Susie, she always likes a glass of wine and she drinks it in such a ladylike manner from a glass.

Susie drank the wine with relish and I sat with her, cradling her head as Neville gave her the lethal injection. Susie slipped away peacefully and Neville took her back to the surgery so her body could be cremated. All I was left with was her collar and memories of my first milking goat. When Graham returned home that evening it was to a very subdued and tearful wife. I was fast realising that working with animals meant walking hand in hand with birth and death. This was something I would have to come to terms with. Susie's demise presented us with a problem; we had a shortage of milk. Angie's kids guzzled all the milk she was able to produce so Graham agreed I should get another milking nanny. I decided to visit the local livestock market in the hope I would find a suitable replacement. Our hens had grown in numbers so I took some with me to sell in the auction. When I arrived at the market I looked at the goats. There were many young kids, a couple of Billies but only one nanny goat. The nanny was pure white, very thin, with long hooves, which urgently needed to be trimmed. As she stood in the pen she had an air of neglect. I ran my hands over her body, each bone was clearly defined. As I felt her full udder she flinched and gave me a wary look. There did not appear to be too much wrong with her that a few square meals and tender loving care would not put right, so I decided to bid for her. The hens were auctioned first and the lot I had entered drew much interest. The bidding was keen and I achieved a very good price. The goat was one of the last animals to be auctioned so I had to be patient. Whilst I was waiting, a gentleman approached me and asked, "I tried to buy those hens you brought but I was outbid. I don't suppose you have any more for sale?"

I replied, "I have, but they are at home."

The man was keen to buy some hens; he explained, "We live in Coventry. Could we follow you home and see the hens?"

I told him that would not be a problem but I could not leave until the goats had been auctioned as I was interested in purchasing one of them. He agreed to wait and went to find his wife to tell her of his plans. At last, the nanny was auctioned. There was little interest in her and I managed to secure the sale at the cost of twenty pounds. I went to settle my bill and the auctioneer gave me a set of pedigree papers; the goat had the grand sounding name of Greystone Hollybush the Second, I named her Holly.

I walked Holly towards my car and was joined by the gentleman and his wife. I was surprised when I saw his wife, the saying 'different as chalk and cheese' sprang immediately to mind! He was dressed in casual clothes and had a down to earth manner. His wife on the oth-

Chapter 21 – Farewell to Susie

er hand, looked as though she had just stepped out from the pages of Vogue magazine. She smiled at me and in a cut glass voice said, "I'm very pleased to meet you."

By now we had reached my car, the man said, "My car is much bigger than yours, we can take the goat home for you." I thought it very kind of the man but one glance at his wife's face told me she did not approve of the offer. I quickly explained, "I don't think that would be a good idea, goats can make an awful mess if they get frightened, I know. It took me a whole afternoon to clean my husband's van after we had transported a goat in it." The smile on the woman's face slipped, her lips pursed as though she had a sour taste in her mouth.

Her expression did not improve when her husband said, "I insist, we will take Holly home."

There was no more I could do; I had warned them and we walked to their car. The car was a huge, brand new, shiny, top of the range estate; Holly would certainly be travelling in style!

The journey home only took twenty minutes, but I knew from the thunderous expression on the wife's face when they arrived, that Holly had done her worst! Sure enough the carpeted interior of the car was covered in urine and much worse! The man was unconcerned and I tried to clean the mess up as best I could. The wife was anxious to leave and said, "Shall we go and see these hens?"

I took them to the poultry house and the woman followed reluctantly, tottering on the grass in her high heels. The man was enthusiastic when he saw the hens and agreed to buy six of them. I sold them at a reduced price, the least I could do as he had saved me the bother of valeting my car. The man looked worried as he said, "I haven't got anything I can transport them in."

"Don't worry, I can find a large sturdy box. We can make some air holes and they will be quite safe until you reach home."

I found a box and put the hens safely inside. We lifted the box into the car and I prepared to say farewell when the wife spoke. "Would it be possible to use your bathroom?"

I agreed readily and took her into the house. She must have performed a complete makeover by the length of time she spent in the bathroom. Finally she emerged, the air filled with the scent of her newly applied perfume. When we returned to the car six faces greeted us. Peering out of the rear window, the hens had escaped from the box! One glance of the interior revealed a careless smattering of bird droppings all over the seats. The man was unperturbed, the woman stared in disbelief. Hurriedly, I said, "I'll put them back in the box, and try and clean the seats."

Calmly the woman said, "There is no need to trouble yourself. I arrived here surrounded by goat droppings, and I shall arrive home surrounded by bird shit."

With great dignity she opened the passenger door. With an unused lace hankie she proceeded to wipe the bird droppings from her seat. She sat down and firmly slammed the door shut. As they left the farm the six heads were still peering from the rear window gazing wistfully at the home they were leaving behind. I often wonder how she coped with the hens scratching and messing in her garden.

In the early evening I went to milk Holly for the first time. I was now well used to the milking game but her reaction to being milked took me by surprise. As I tried to milk her she kicked at my hands relentlessly, until she had managed to graze the skin on my knuckles. I talked to her kindly but she repeated the process the next morning. I wondered if she had something wrong with her udder so I asked the vet to call. Neville arrived and I took him to meet Holly. She took one look at him and charged forward with her head down. With great difficulty, Neville examined her and said, "I can't find anything wrong with the udder but I think she has been milked roughly in the past and that is why she is behaving in this manner." It took many weeks before Holly would stand still whilst she was being milked but one thing never altered – she hated men and the sight of one would send her into charge mode! I can only assume at some time a man had treated her badly. I was fortunate Holly had accepted me but this tolerance did not stretch to other family members.

.

Chapter 22
Chantey to the Rescue

As the builders continued to work on the farm they became interested in the animals. The geese and hens benefited from their presence as the men shared their packed lunches with the birds. One lunch time Gerry came to find me, he was worried. He said, "There is something wrong with the cockerel, he won't share my lunch, all he does is cluck loudly and keep running away."

As Gerry was so concerned I decided to investigate. As soon as Chantey saw me he began clucking wildly, running towards me and then away from me. I followed him, hoping I would be able to catch him and see what was causing him so much concern. At last he reached the hedge and Chantey stood still, I approached ready to pick him up when I saw one of the hens trapped in some wire at the bottom of the hedge. It was easy to release the bird and she ran off unharmed, with Chantey in hot pursuit; they made their way to the builders and managed to devour the last crumbs of lunch.

I believed the incident with Chantey was coincidental, he couldn't really have been asking for help, could he? Some weeks later I had my answer. I was busy working on the farm when Chantey repeated his agitated dance, jokingly I said, "Come on old fellow, show me what's wrong."

Chantey led me to the hen house and stood by one of the nest boxes. In the gloom I peered inside, curled up asleep was a ginger cat. I had not seen the cat before, and I wondered as the hen coop was near the road if a car had injured him. I carefully stroked the cat, he opened his eyes and slowly stretched his legs as he awakened. Chantey glowered at the squatter, I picked the cat up and took him out of Chantey's home. Whilst in my arms the cat purred loudly. I told him, "You can stay if you want but not in my rooster's house, he doesn't like it." The cat must have understood me, as he never ventured in to the hen house again, but stay on the farm he did. The cat organised his own sleeping arrangements, he shunned the warm barn and chose instead to sleep in an old bin. As the days progressed he showed no sign of wanting to leave and so I gave him a name. Joe and Lucy enjoyed watching a cartoon series entitled Top Cat, the feline character lived in a dustbin, so our ginger guest became known as TC.

As is typical of a cat, TC had chosen his home and within days was completely settled. He was a very affectionate cat. He loved Joe and Lucy, and wherever I worked on the farm he would be beside me. I often wonder how he came to be a stray because I am sure he was someone's much loved pet. Within weeks he had made the farm his kingdom. He lived in harmony with the birds, never raising a claw to defenceless chicks. He was fearless too, if a horse should dare to sniff him it would be rewarded with a swift slap on its nose. TC lived his life on the farm, never venturing into the house. He was the first of a motley assortment of cats who would find sanctuary on the farm in the future years.

Chapter 23
Trying the Gypsy Lifestyle

September was fast approaching. New specialist workmen arrived at the farm. Among them carpenters who would construct the roof. Building was soon to start on the existing house and it was time for us to move out. Graham had purchased a mobile home and the day arrived when it was delivered. It was so large a crane was hired to lift it over the hedge and place it on the lawn. Graham and I went to examine what was going to be our home for the next four weeks. Graham surveyed his 'bargain' with pride. I was unimpressed! It was very basic, with four rooms, a portable loo and an air of abandonment. Doris and I set to, attempting to make it habitable, but four weeks living in this tin can were going to seem like a lifetime! Joe and Lucy thought it was a big adventure and enjoyed the prospect of the gypsy life. We filled the caravan with our belongings and moved in. We soon discovered our new home had a few extras built in. All four of us began to suffer from itchy lumps which I soon diagnosed as fleabites! The van had to be fumigated but it was some days before we could rid it completely of unwanted guests.

Life in the caravan was very basic; we only had cold running water, a coal fire, and thankfully, a supply of electricity from the house. Fred and Rose were delighted with our frequent visits but our welcome began to wear thin when we used all their hot water for baths. Graham began to work even longer hours. Office life was preferable to living in the caravan. I contented myself with the knowledge it would not be for long. However, once we had vacated the house, the building progress seemed to slow down. Graham decided I was in need of a break and arranged a night away in a hotel. Peggy agreed to run the farm in our absence.

We left home on the Thursday morning. I busied myself with last minute instructions for Peggy. Just before we departed, the owner of Bo, the palomino horse, came to see me. She asked, "Could I use your phone, I'm worried about Bo. He has developed a cough." I told her to go ahead. Graham became impatient to leave he said, "Come on Ann, let's get going before someone else wants something." I was eager to leave, it had been a long time since I had enjoyed the luxury of visiting a hotel. For the next twenty-four hours I would have no washing up or cooking to do.

I was not disappointed with the hotel. Unfortunately, the time sped by and all too soon it was time to return to our building site. We arrived home late Friday afternoon. Peggy was pacing up and down the drive. The moment I saw her agitated state I knew something was badly wrong. No sooner had I climbed out of the car than Peggy ran to meet me. "Thank goodness you're home, I don't know what to do." She declared.

"Calm down," I said. "What has happened?"

The words came tumbling out as Peggy between sobs said, "You know that Bo had a cough, well the vet arrived earlier and gave him an injection, and they think he is dead." Sternly I said, " Who thinks he is dead?"

Peggy replied, "The vet and Bo's owner, they are in the caravan. You had better talk to them." I opened the caravan door and saw the distraught owner and beside her a young woman who was equally upset. The owner sprang to her feet and begged, "Ann please help, I think Bo is dead."

Perplexed I said, "Don't you know if he is alive or dead?"

The young woman stood up. Trembling, she said, " I'm the vet, I was just giving him a routine injection and he collapsed. I've only just qualified; this is my first visit and I don't know what to do."

In a matter-of-fact voice I said, "We had better go and find out whether he is dead or not." The vet shouted hysterically, "I can't go back to the stable, take my stethoscope and see if there is a heart beat."

Chapter 23 – Trying the Gypsy Lifestyle

Angrily, I said, "It's no use giving me that, I haven't been trained to use one, but I do know a dead animal when I see one. I'll go and see him." I walked in to his stable and in the far corner Bo lay still. I touched the warm body but I could not detect any signs of life. I examined his eyes, there was no reflex, and I didn't need to be a vet to know life was extinct.

I returned to the caravan, Graham was sitting with the women doing his best to console them. They eagerly searched my face for news, my expression confirmed their worst fears. "I'm sorry," I said. "But Bo is definitely dead, I checked his eye reflex." The moment I had spoken the vet stood up, ran to the door and said, "I can't cope with this. I shall have to leave." With that she left us. I turned to the owner and gently asked, "What do you want to do now?"

Amidst tears she said, "Can you deal with it?"

Sadly I replied, "Yes, but do you want a post mortem performed as I think the vet may have been negligent, certainly her response has not been professional."

With a heavy heart she said, "Nothing will bring Bo back, please arrange for the knackers man to take him."

The owner left and I phoned the local knackers man who said he would be with us shortly. Peggy agreed to stay and look after the children while Graham and I awaited his arrival. The builders left as they had finished their day's work but two carpenters continued to work late. The carpenters were brothers, both young men, the eldest was called Paul and the younger was named Andy. Eventually, a plain white lorry drew into the Farm. It was the knacker's man. He was in his fifties, well-built and accustomed to dealing with carcasses. He got out of the lorry and asked, "Where is the body?" We took him to the stable and showed him the still body.

He stood assessing the situation and said, "The horse is in an awkward place, I won't be able to winch him onto the lorry. I suggest we take the front off the stable."

Graham, when he spoke was adamant, "We're not taking the front off this stable. It will damage the building permanently. I suggest we move him towards the door and then you can attach the winch."

The man tersely replied, "I don't think you understand the situation fully. That is a ton dead weight, the three of us will not be able to move him. We might be able to do it if we had some extra man power." I thought quickly. Peggy couldn't help us. She was already very upset and if I asked her to move a dead horse I knew she would resign first. Then inspiration dawned, "Graham what about asking Paul and Andy?"

They are still here." Graham was determined the stable would stay intact so he said, "Go and ask them."

I quickly found them and said, "We have got a problem, the knackers man has come for the horse which died earlier; he says we can't get the horse out of the stable without taking the front off. Graham won't agree to it. Between them they think we can drag the horse to the door and then we will be able to get him out. The problem is we need some extra muscle. Is there any chance you could help us?"

The brothers looked at each other, then Paul spoke, "This isn't a wind up is it?"

"I wish it were" I said dispiritedly, "We really do need your help."

Paul said, "You can count me in, I'm not very keen on the idea but I can see you are in trouble." Andy followed his brother's lead and agreed to help. We went to the stable and put our backs into the task at hand. It was hard work, but slowly we managed to steer the body towards the door. The rest was easy, the horse was winched on to the lorry and Bo set off on his final journey. Graham, the brothers and I went to the caravan and I made us all a cup of tea. I thanked Paul and Andy. Andy said, "I've never done anything like that before, at least I shall have a tale to tell in the pub."

I don't know what tales he told in the pub but I heard him the next morning recounting the event to the other builders who sat silently with disbelief. Nor do I know why Bo died, the vet very soon afterwards resigned from her position. The owner never replaced her beloved Bo. We did not let the stable again as we had decided to use the stables as they became vacant for our ever expanding population of goats and pigs.

Chapter 24
Home Produced Meat

September had passed and October arrived, but the building work was nowhere near completion. It was clear that we would have to remain in the caravan a while longer. By now Gertie's piglets were growing rapidly, all nine had survived and I sold seven of them to a local man who wanted to fatten them. I was left with two weaners, which were almost ready for slaughter. Graham watched their progress keenly, unlike me he was looking forward to home produced pork. I knew if I was to continue to keep farm animals I would have to accept they would be slaughtered so I decided to make the whole process as stress free as possible for the animals. I found a local slaughterhouse, only ten minutes from home, which I then went and visited. I met the staff and was confident they would treat my animals with respect and carry out the job professionally. The day eventually dawned when Graham took the weaners on their final journey. Two days later I collected the neatly parcelled joints of meat. When I had first embarked on the venture Bert offered these words of wisdom, "Anna, don't give any animal you are going to eat a name; otherwise you will never be able to kill it. I suggest when you sit down to a meal of your own produced meat pour yourself a couple of glasses of wine first and then it won't be so difficult." The time had come, as I grilled the pork chops I poured myself liberal helpings of sherry. Bert was quite right I was hardly aware of what I was eating! It may have taken more than two glasses but I had done it and there was no going back. Graham was delighted, " This pork was delicious" he said, " It has really got flavour. When will you mate Gertie again?"

I replied, "When she next comes into season I will take her back to the boar."

It was not long before Gertie was ready for mating, I rang Dennis and he agreed that she could return to the boar. As I was transporting the farm animals regularly, I had invested in a livestock trailer. All I had to do was to persuade Gertie to climb on board; easier said than done! Graham and I tried to cajole her on to the ramp, but she would have none of it. Twelve packets of cheese and onion crisps, and constant tummy scratching finally did the trick. Gertie was off on honeymoon.

We arrived at Dennis's farm; I wondered what he would think of Gertie as he had not seen her for some months, I remembered his warning about ruining her, I hoped he would be impressed. There was no problem getting her out of the trailer. She happily sauntered in to the boar's abode. Dennis said little until we were ready to leave, then he spoke, "Don't expect that pig to look as good when you fetch her back; she might get the odd skin graze from her tussles with the boar." He said no more. But my body was filled with pride. Obviously, Dennis thought I had looked after her well but that was the nearest he would come to giving praise!

Some days later I returned alone to collect Gertie. Dennis offered me a cup of tea. I sat surrounded by his cats and dogs, in the corner cage the Barn Owl continued to stare in his sagacious way. We chatted companionably, I hoped one day that I could acquire some of his knowledge and experience which he had gained through a lifetime of farming. I was curious why he should have a Barn Owl and I ventured to ask why? He replied, "I've got a few birds of prey, they are magnificent animals, the rest I keep outside. This one I keep in here to get rid of unwanted visitors." Puzzled, I asked, "How does that work?"

"Simple," he replied. "I let him out of the cage and he attacks any stranger." I hurriedly finished my tea and collected Gertie. Over the years I never out stayed my welcome so was spared the attentions of the Owl. I had discovered that Dennis and I shared another interest; I was fascinated by birds of prey. I dreamed one day of owning a Lan-

Chapter 24 – Home Produced Meat

ner Falcon. It was still a dream and Graham remained in blissful ignorance.

Chapter 25
Luck Runs Out

October was drawing to a close and we still resided in the caravan. Graham decided it was time to take drastic action; we moved back into the house and lived in one room, the lounge. The builders found our presence an encumbrance and speeded up their work. Even though life was difficult staying in the house, I found it preferable to our existence in the caravan. The holiday season was at an end, so there were fewer cats to care for. Since the cattery had opened I had looked after many cats, all without incident but my luck was about to run out.

Mr. and Mrs. Pretty had left in my care their elderly cat Ben. He was the perfect guest, a gentle, jet black, affectionate cat. He had undergone surgery earlier in the year to remove a cancerous growth. The operation had been a success, but his owners were concerned about leaving him, so decided to phone at intervals to enquire about his health. The first week I was able to tell them he was perfectly fit and eating well, but at the start of the second week of his holiday, events took a turn for the worse.

One morning I took Ben his breakfast, but instead of greeting me, he continued to lie in his bed. He was not interested in his food and he had an air of dejection. Over the few short years I had worked with animals I had learnt a great deal, I have been blessed with an instinctive knowledge when something is not as it should be. Many times I have visited vets and said, "I don't know what is wrong but I've got a gut feeling about this one." Rarely does this 'feeling' let me

Chapter 25 - Luck Runs Out

down and vets have come to dread those words as it usually means they are presented with a difficult case.

Ben's case was no exception, the cancer had not returned but his kidneys were failing and his prospects looked bleak. Over the next two days we fought to stop the degeneration of his kidneys but it was to no avail. Ben was tired of life and the vet decided the only humane option was euthanasia. I agreed, but I didn't want to give permission. I asked if we could wait one more day, as it was likely his owners would phone for a progress report. It was agreed, and I hoped that Mr. and Mrs. Pretty would ring. I was not disappointed, they contacted me that evening and I was able to tell them of Ben's plight. They would not allow Ben to suffer and asked if I would be with him when he was put to sleep, this I did.

Throughout the years incidents such as Ben have sadly been repeated. Many of the cats I board today have been visiting me regularly for over fifteen years and are now in their twilight years. Occasionally, I am present at the end. It does not become any easier but I have learnt how to cope with it. When owners lose a beloved pet they grieve and I have to be there for them as well, offering a listening ear and words of comfort. On their return from holiday Mr. and Mrs. Pretty visited me. They thanked me for caring for Ben and gave me a sculpture of a Kestrel, which to this day has a place of pride in my living room.

The cattery was well established, and so was my reputation as an oracle about cats. My customers would ring up with all manner of questions, and sometimes people I had not met, rang for advice. Many owners had cats with behavioural problems, others wanted general information about different breeds of cat. One evening the phone rang, it was a customer. She said, "One of my cats has been run over and I think it is dead. What should I do?"

I asked, "Where is the cat?"

Quickly she replied, "It's still outside on the verge, neither my husband nor I, can bear to go and look, a neighbour has told us he is lying there."

Sharply I said, "You must go and look, he may be unconscious and in shock. If you leave him there he will die. If he is alive roll him onto a blanket, keep him warm and get him to an emergency vet."

Life on the Funny Farm

She agreed to follow my instructions, and phoned the next day to inform me the cat was alive and would make a full recovery.

With the cattery well established, many of our customers bemoaned the fact that they could not board their dogs with us; Graham and I saw it as a natural progression that we should venture into boarding kennels. Plans were drawn up for seventeen kennels and we began the long process once again, of applying for planning permission. Christmas was approaching with speed, the family were expecting to stay as usual, but as December dawned the builders were still in residence. The run up to Christmas was chaotic, industrial heaters were working overtime, drying out the newly plastered walls ready for the decorators. With a week to go the Turkeys were killed and dressed, I had managed to rear all the birds and the surplus I placed in my freezer to be used throughout the year. At last, the decorators finished. It was time for the carpets to be laid.

Five days before the family were due to stay the carpet fitters arrived. Rolls of floor coverings were unloaded from the van, and then disaster struck! Doris was helping me to bring order to the house when we heard the sound of running water. At first I was unconcerned I said, "The builders must have plumbed in the new bathroom upstairs." Doris decided to go and look. Within seconds I heard her high pitched scream. I ran to her and we met at the bottom of the stairs. The new, bare wooden staircase resembled Niagara Falls as water cascaded from the loft. All hell broke loose, builders began rushing to and fro; the tank in the roof had overflowed due to a malfunction. Eventually the flow of water was stopped, but not before gallons of water flooded the bare floors. It had become impossible to lay the carpets, the men departed, only to return on Christmas Eve when the floors had dried out. As the family began to arrive they were greeted by an assortment of builders and craftsmen leaving the farm, their work finally complete.

Chapter 26
Surprise Announcement

Christmas lunch brought added stress; not only was I head chef but I had produced the Turkey and Pork on offer. The family devoured their meal with relish, the home produced meat was a great success. When the meal was finished we sat around the table engrossed in conversation. Graham decided the time was right for him to make an announcement, he began. "The firm has done well this year, but in business you have to keep moving forward otherwise your competitors will overtake you. I have decided to expand and open a depot in London." My heart sank, I asked, "You are not suggesting that we should move are you?"

Graham was quick to allay my fears, "No. There is no need. The depot will be a subsidiary. Birmingham will remain the Head Office. However, I shall have to spend a lot of time setting up the new branch. I have found suitable premises. It will necessitate me living in London during the week and commuting home at weekends." I did not welcome the idea but it was preferable to moving house. Graham had always supported me in my endeavours and now the roles would be reversed.

The planned expansion of the firm gathered momentum. In a couple of months Graham would begin life as a commuter. As the plans neared fruition Graham voiced his concern, "Ann, I'm worried about you being alone during the evenings, it isn't as though you have any neighbours for support."

Confidently I replied, "There's no need to worry, the children are here so I won't be lonely. I've got Sally, the dog as protection."

Graham laughed, "I don't think Sally is much good, she is more likely to lick someone to death rather than bite them." I knew he had a point but I failed to see a way to allay his concern. My loving husband suggested, "I think we should have a trained guard dog. I've done some research and there is a kennel nearby which specialises in training dogs for security purposes."

I liked the idea of another canine companion but I voiced my worries, "Would the children be safe with a dog like that?" Graham smiled, "I have booked an appointment at the training centre, we can meet the staff and the dogs they think would be suitable. I have explained we have two young children. There is no harm in at least going to look, is there?"

I agreed to the visit and a week later found us in a huge building with various dogs being put through their paces.

The dogs were German Shepherds at various stages of their training. All the dogs were large, majestic creatures with an air of nobility. One by one the dogs performed an obedience test displaying their skills. I met each dog individually, they were so similar it was difficult to decide which one was best for us. I looked into their eyes, searching for a clue. Most returned my gaze with an indifferent stare. One bold, big, beautiful dog stood considering me, his brown liquid eyes revealed gentleness, he led my hand and I made my decision. I said to the handler, "This is the one for me." The handler was a big, burly man, called Rob. He was very down to earth and stood no nonsense from the dogs or the prospective owners. He said, "That dog will suit you well, he is called Zac. He is eighteen months old, we trained him and his brother as bomb dogs. His brother is now working at Sri Lanka airport. I'm afraid Zac failed the bomb course."

"Why did he fail?" I enquired.

Rob explained, "To test their suitability we place a number of devices around a room with the scent of explosives, a good dog will find the bomb and communicate this to its handler. Zac was very good at sniffing out the devices but he would rush in and touch the 'bomb', this in turn set off an alarm. Had it been the real thing everything would have been blown to bits."

Chapter 26 – Surprise Announcement

The fact he had failed the bomb course did not matter. I asked, "How soon can we have him?"

Rob replied, "Zac is a highly trained dog, he has been taught to the highest standard. He can even apprehend a running criminal. You, on the other hand, have no training. You can come back next week and I will teach you how to become his handler. You can then take him away with you but you must return every week until Zac accepts you as his new pack leader."

"How long will it take?" I asked.

"That depends on you and the dog, it can take a couple of months." He replied.

Chapter 27
One Woman and a Dog

A few days later I attended my lesson. Zac had been taught numerous commands. To ensure the dog would only obey the handler his commands were in code, for instance if I wanted him to leave, I used the word table. I had a list of words to memorise but after our long training session we were allowed to leave as a raw team. Zac settled in to his new home easily, he became firm friends with Sally, and each day I spent time practising our training. A week later I returned for more tuition. I let Zac out of the car and as soon as he saw Rob he ran hell for leather towards him, not giving me a backward glance. I felt hurt as Zac greeted his original pack leader with boundless joy. The lesson did not go well, the dog ignored my commands and Rob shouted in frustration, "There is nothing wrong with the dog, stop pissing about and get control." I was furious; who did this man think he was? How dare he speak to me like that, but I knew I was letting the dog down, I was thankful when the lesson was over.

Zac and I returned to the farm and for the next week we continued to practice, all too soon our next lesson arrived. As soon as I let the dog out of the car he ran with gay, reckless abandonment towards Rob. The lesson was a slight improvement on the previous week but Rob still managed to make me feel inadequate. I began to dread our training sessions under the eagle eye of Rob. At home Zac and I worked well together but in Rob's presence it all fell apart.

I had been attending the lessons for six weeks and had begun to wonder if Zac would ever accept me as his handler. On our seventh

Chapter 27 – One Woman and a Dog

lesson I let Zac out of the car and true to form he ran at full gallop towards his beloved master. He greeted Rob with delight and then turned and ran towards me, and sat obediently at my side. Rob called him back and Zac turned his head in his direction but then continued to look towards me for instructions. Rob repeatedly called him, but Zac was not budging from my side. Rob joined us and said, "There is no lesson today, he is your dog now. He has accepted you as his handler and pack leader. Keep on working with him and you will make a good team." I was so pleased Zac had finally given me his allegiance.

Zac quickly became one of the family and wherever I was working he would be at my side. I trusted him completely and when it was time for Graham to begin his work in London I knew the children and I would be safe in his care. Zac soon gave me a demonstration of his loyalty. We needed some electrical work done and our regular electrician, Tim, paid us a visit. The problem necessitated Tim climbing the ladder into the loft space. Zac and I left him to his work. Later I went to see how Tim was progressing with the work, I stood at the bottom of the ladder and shouted, "How is it going? I'm making a cup of tea would you like one?"

Tim came to the hatch and peered down, he said, "I'd love a cuppa, I'll come down."

He began the descent when the screwdriver he was carrying fell from his grasp and scored a direct hit to my shoulder. The sudden pain caused me to cry out, Zac left my side and climbed swiftly up the ladder closing his powerful jaws around Tim's leg.

A terrified Tim shouted, "Call him off, be quick about it."

Everything had happened so quickly, my mind was a complete blank I said, "I can't remember which command to use." Zac had a firm grasp of the leg, Tim was trapped on the ladder, he shouted, "Don't just stand there, bloody well remember the word." Tim's predicament jolted my memory and I called Zac off his quarry. The dog obediently descended the ladder and picked the screwdriver up, and held it tightly between his teeth. Tim nervously climbed down and Zac still holding his trophy stared at him. Tim said, "As far as I'm concerned he can keep the screwdriver, but it has a glass handle, and he could damage himself. But I'm not taking it away from him." Zac willingly gave me the offending article, and I checked Tim's leg wondering what damage had been done, but there wasn't a

Life on the Funny Farm

mark. My canine protector had followed his training to the last letter. I knew beyond any doubt whilst Zac was around there was no need to worry about our safety.

Chapter 28
The Dog Hotel Opens

It was strange Graham not being at home during the week but I had plenty to keep me occupied. Spring was fast approaching; the cattery would soon be busy again with the holiday season arriving. Gertie was expecting another litter of piglets, as usual there were kittens in the house, and the plans had been accepted for the kennels. Building work on the canine hotel began. As soon as we received permission and if all went well we would be open for the beginning of May. Many of the builders who had worked on the house returned and worked around the clock to meet the deadline for our opening. This time they kept to their schedule and our first canine guests arrived on the first of May.

Life was hectic and now we had the added work of the kennels, I needed more staff. The number of horses stabled at the farm had decreased but amongst those which remained was Fleur. Her owner, Jenny had become a good friend. She was very interested in dogs. Not only did she breed them but she was also a highly respected judge of the Hungarian Puli breed. She worked part time for a local vet, I was delighted when she told me she had given up the job and would like to work in the kennels two days a week. It was wonderful to have such an experienced person as a member of the team but we needed a full time member of staff as well. At the weekends we had a number of students who helped out, and one of these was a girl was called Gemma. She was a tall, thin girl who resembled a marathon runner. She was very hard working and adored the animals. She came to me one day and said, "I have decided I want to have a career in the anim-

Life on the Funny Farm

al sector, would there be an opening here for me?" It was the answer to my prayers; she was willing and eager to learn. She liked working with all the different species on the farm; the situation was ideal. I offered her the job, on the understanding she would attend college on day release for two years, by which time she would have a qualification in small animal care. Gemma was delighted and accepted the offer eagerly. It was a decision neither of us would come to regret.

Chapter 29
Bill and Minnie

As the summer progressed Meg and I attended many cat shows. Meg showed her Chinchilla stud cat called Ziggy, whilst I took my Burmese along. At one of the shows we saw a new breed of cat on exhibition, it was a Burmilla. Some years earlier there had been an accidental mating of a Chinchilla and Burmese, the result was a very impressive, large, silvery tipped cat. Meg and I were in total agreement the result was stunning. A group of breeders were now trying to get the Burmilla breed recognised. Enthusiastically I said, "Meg we could have a go at breeding Burmillas, I could send one of my Burmese to Ziggy, and in return Bill could mate one of your Chinchilla girls."

Meg needed no time to consider the proposition. She was completely smitten, swiftly she answered, "I think that's a great idea, as soon as we have a girl ready to mate we will go ahead." We did not have to wait long, Bluebell came into call and I took her to visit her new bridegroom. It was love at first sight, and the two of them spent a passionate few days together. No sooner was Bluebell home, than Meg rang to say Minnie, her Chinchilla, was calling. Minutes later Meg arrived with her beautiful aristocratic cat. We took her to meet Bill; as usual he was very enthusiastic and mated her straight away. They were quite happy in each other's company but sometimes this is not the case and I have to separate them at night when they are not supervised. Before going to bed I checked the honeymooners, they were curled up together in bed so I left them to a night of passion.

Life on the Funny Farm

Next morning I awoke and visited the stud house. As usual, Bill ran to greet me, his feet and mouth were full of white silky fur. My stomach churned, had he attacked Minnie or worse still, killed her? I rushed in to the pen and yanked the door open, the floor was covered in a white down. Hurriedly I scanned the pen, in the far corner in the litter tray sat a forlorn Minnie. She was alive but naked! The only fur remaining on her body was on her head and tail, the rest was scattered around the stud house. Throughout the night Bill had systematically removed her beautiful flowing locks. Amazingly, there was not a mark on her body. The relief she was alive soon evaporated when I realised I would have to tell Meg what had befallen her beloved cat. There was no point in postponing the moment. I went inside and phoned, "Hello Meg." I nervously began, "Minnie is alright in herself but there has been a bit of an accident."

Meg snapped, "What do you mean by an accident?"

The words came out in a rush, "I don't think Bill liked mating a long haired cat, it is the first one he has ever met. It seems he spent the night plucking out her fur."

I could hear Meg's sigh of relief as she said, "Don't worry if she has the odd bit of fur missing it will soon grow back."

"I don't think you quite understand, the only fur she has left is on her head and tail." Before I could explain further Meg shouted down the phone, "I'm coming round straight away to collect her." I replaced the receiver and sadly contemplated the end of a beautiful friendship, Bill had a lot to answer for.

Within minutes Meg arrived, I had swept up the ravaged fur and placed it in a carrier bag. Meg was distinctly cool in manner as we walked towards the stud house. When she saw Minnie I expected her to explode, but instead she collapsed into a fit of uncontrollable laughter. I wasn't sure whether to laugh or cry, but Meg turned towards me and said, "You must see the funny side, no one would believe this."

Until that moment I had not found it remotely funny, but with our friendship still intact I joined in the laughter. Meg took Minnie home. As she was leaving I gave her the bag of fur. Smiling, I said, "Perhaps you could stick it back on!" Nine weeks later Bluebell gave birth to a litter of six sensational first generation Burmillas. Sadly, Minnie was not pregnant, nor did she ever call again. One night with

Chapter 27 – One Woman and a Dog

Bill put her off sex forever! I gave Meg the pick of Bluebell's litter as some recompense for Minnie's night of domestic violence.

Chapter 30
Doris Bows Out

Life on the farm was hectic. I had little spare time to brood about Graham working in London. My own animal family and our four legged guests kept me well and truly occupied. I had a small band of competent staff but nothing stays the same forever. Doris became ill and the diagnosis was heart trouble. It was not life threatening, but she would have to take things much easier and so I lost not only an excellent cleaner, but someone whom I could rely on. I doubted I would find anyone to match her, but I need not have worried. Peggy suggested her mother would like the job. Peggy's mum, Gwyn was in her early fifties, an attractive lady who liked children. But apart from owning a cat she did not share her daughter's passion for animals. My home was filled with cats and dogs, sometimes a sick bird, kid goat, or piglet would also be in residence. It took quite a few weeks for Gwyn to acclimatise herself to the strange household, but she persevered. Only one thing really gave her cause for concern and she could not keep it secret for any longer. "Ann," she began, "I don't mind the mud, bits of straw, litter trays everywhere but I keep finding these things scattered around the house."

She opened her hand, inside was one of the favourite toys of my Burmese cats, a rabbit's foot. The cats adored them and at each show I would buy them a bagful, they played with them for hours, and eventually they disappeared. I assume they ate them.

Chapter 27 – One Woman and a Dog

I looked up at Gwyn and said, "It's a rabbits foot, and the cats love them."

Tersely, Gwyn replied, "I know what it is. I don't like touching them. They are everywhere." From the tone in her voice I realised I had to make a choice between keeping my cats happy or losing a cleaner. I didn't want to lose Gwyn, nor did I wish to upset my cats. I suggested, "How about I go round the house before you arrive and pick up all the feet I can find, would that make you happier?"

Gwyn smiled, "You can try but I doubt you will find them all." It was agreed. From then on, I went on a rabbit foot hunt before my cleaner arrived for work. Sometimes I did miss one, but Gwyn never complained again and we worked happily together for many years.

No sooner had I solved the problem of a cleaner than Peggy announced she was leaving. The eighteen-year old I had employed years earlier, was now a young woman in love. Her husband to be was leaving the area, taking Peggy with him. We had spent many happy hours together and I knew I would miss her. We did not throw a party, or go out for a meal. Instead, we visited the local livestock market. We had done this numerous times before, bringing all manner of birds home, but this would be our last visit together. I had not planned to buy anything, but Peggy and I were in for a surprise.

Chapter 31
Anthony and Cleopatra

As we wandered around the market a tall, distinguished-looking gentleman crossed our path. Under his arm he carried a large cardboard box. Trailing from a hole neatly cut in the end of the box was a bouquet of peacock feathers. Before either of us could speak the feathers began to move. I was enthralled. Excitedly, I said, "He's got a peacock in there. I wonder if it is for sale?" Without hesitation I chased after the stranger. Without any introduction I asked, "Are you selling the peacock?"

The gentleman explained, "I have arranged to meet someone who is buying this bird and his mate. I only have one pair, are you interested in peafowl?"

I tried to hide the disappointment from my voice, "I would have been very interested, they would have looked great on my farm. If you ever have any in the future would you let me know, I'll give you my phone number." The man agreed, we continued on our way. We went to the auction but did not purchase anything. Peggy knew the birds I really wanted were beyond my reach, and with a resigned air we headed towards the exit. "Oi you," a voice boomed. "Wait a minute." We turned round to see our peacock seller running towards us. We waited, the man between gasps for breath said, "The people never turned up for the birds, you can have them if you want. They'll cost you fifty quid." This was an opportunity too good to miss, I rifled through my purse, only to find I was five pounds short. Peggy, bless her heart, tipped the contents of her money bag out and man-

Chapter 31 – Anthony and Cleopatra

aged to scrape together the other fiver. I paid the man. Into my hand he pressed a pound coin. "Have that as your luck money, Lady." This was the first time I encountered this custom. When purchasing any animal, farmers of the old school return a small amount of money to the buyer to bring them luck with the animal. Sadly, this custom is dying out.

We collected the birds from the gentleman's van and transferred them to my car. After the short journey home we released them into a stable for the time being. The peacock looked magnificent, the peahen in comparison was a dowdy bird, but immediately it was clear they were attached to each other. I did not have to think very hard to find them suitable names. From then on they were Anthony and Cleopatra.

Within a few days they were free on the farm. Anthony spent hours courting his girl, his tail spread out showing all its glory. If that was not sufficient to attract Cleopatra's attention he would shimmy his tail feathers in the best ballroom style. This in turn would make a soothing rattling sound. With Cleo's interest aroused, Anthony would let out a loud whooping noise and set off in hot pursuit of his coy lover. The courtship ritual never ceases to enthral me, nor the intricacies of the tail feathers. The wonderful colours, the detailed 'eye' on each feather are a testament to the wonder of nature. Until I owned peafowl I had only experienced them at stately homes and then, more often than not, they refused to display their artistry. The customers found them fascinating; they were certainly an attraction, but not everyone shared my enthusiasm! As usual Graham came home at the weekend, I could not wait to show him my latest acquisition, but as it was dark I would have to wait until the morning. I decided to say nothing and surprise my husband. Anthony and Cleopatra treated the farm as their realm, at night they roosted on the rooftop of the house, safe from the clutches of Brer Fox. Graham was tired when he arrived home so it was not long before we retired to bed. Sleep came quickly, and so did wakefulness! In the early hours dawn slowly began to break. Birds seem to be aware of the approach of dawn long before humans. In the summer months the dawn chorus begins at four am. My sleep was abruptly interrupted by Graham violently shaking my body, "Ann, for God's sake wake up. Someone's being murdered out there." Within seconds I was alert, "What do you mean?" I asked.

Graham gabbled, "I was asleep, but I was woken by a dreadful scream, I think someone has been attacked. I think we should call the police."

I had an uncomfortable feeling that I knew who had orchestrated the scream. Slowly I asked, "Did It sound like this?" Upon which I let out a scream of 'My eyeee'

Graham was puzzled, "That's it, how did you know?"

Hesitantly, I said, "Well it was meant to be a surprise, but I have bought a peacock and peahen, at night they roost on the roof just above our bedroom. They must have woken up. The first time I heard the peacock I thought one of the children had hurt their eye and were calling for me. I even rushed into the house, only to find everything was all right. Later on I heard the sound again and realised it was the bird." Graham's face had that usual look of disbelief; the distant tone of his voice was all too familiar as well. "Well, it was a bloody surprise alright! What the hell do we need a peacock for?"

Patiently I replied, "They look so pretty and they are a big hit with the customers. You wait till you see Anthony when he is displaying his tail."

Curtly he said, "If he wakes me up again he won't live to lift his tail."

Oh dear, yet another of my animals had got off on the wrong foot with my husband. True to form, Graham shared my pleasure of Anthony's displays. Like me he got used to them roosting outside the bedroom and their vocalisations did not continue to wake us. The same could not be said for guests who stayed overnight, many thought living near Heathrow Airport would be preferable.

Anthony made a spectacular addition to the farm, and as the weeks progressed he displayed real character. He was a very friendly bird but he disliked the dustmen intensely. Each week when they arrived he would stand over them in a threatening manner, as they departed he would pursue the dustcart down the lane. The first time it happened I chased after him, fearing he would fly away, but he always returned to his ladylove. The dustmen were well used to our aggress-

Chapter 31 - Anthony and Cleopatra

ive geese, and only found Anthony's antics amusing. After many weeks he gave up chasing the lorry and turned his attentions to the tanker, which emptied our septic tank. Fortunately, they only paid periodic visits. I do not know for certain what attracted him to the vehicles but both lorries were bright yellow and I always assumed it was the colour that changed our peacock into a roadrunner!

Chapter 32
Lot 39

The balmy days of mid summer had arrived. Gertie had yet again produced a litter of nine healthy piglets with complete ease. Soon it would be time to castrate the boars and cut their teeth. This time I would make no mistakes, Gertie would be safely under lock and key when the vet came to call. The cattery and kennels were fully booked. Everyone was busy catering for every whim of the animals. As yet I had not found anyone suitable to replace Peggy. The matter needed to be addressed quickly, then fate stepped in. Joe had become firm friends with a local boy, and as is the way of things I had become friendly with his mother, Liz. One day whilst we were talking Liz asked, "Do you know anyone locally who is looking to employ someone part time?" I was hesitant, Liz was a friend and I might end up losing her friendship if I became her boss. On the other hand, the staff I had employed so far had all become my friends, so why shouldn't it work in reverse?" After a short silence I replied,

"I need someone to work in the kennels. You could give it a try, but it is not glamorous work."

Liz answered immediately, "I was hoping you might have something; don't worry about the work. I'm used to cleaning up after my own dogs. I have to muck out my horse as well. There is just one thing, I've never had anything to do with cats, I don't think I could work with them."

Chapter 32 – Lot 39

With relief, I said, "You don't need to worry about the cats, we'll soon convert you."

Liz began work the next week and proved to be an invaluable member of staff. Within a couple of months she gained confidence around my cats and before long there wasn't an animal on the farm she couldn't cope with.

With a full quota of staff I was able to take the odd day off from work. I tried to leave my weekends free, as this was when Graham was at home, but occasionally I attended a cat show with Meg. One morning Meg called, and over coffee asked, "Any chance you could be free next Saturday?" I assumed she wanted to exhibit her cat somewhere, happily I replied, "Yes, where do you want to go?"

Full of enthusiasm, Meg said, "You know I have been thinking about getting a horse. Throughout my childhood I had a pony. Now I miss riding. There is a horse sale next weekend and I wondered if you would take me?" A horse sale was the last thing I expected but I could see no harm in going along, so the date was agreed. When Graham returned home on the Friday evening I told him where I was going the next day. My husband was far from pleased, he said, "Can't Meg go on her own?"

I replied, "You know she has no transport, anyway she would like the company. I don't see what you are bothered about; I shall only be away a few hours. I put up with you being absent all week."

Sharply Graham said, "I don't mind you being away. I'm just worried what you will bring home with you."

I began to smile, "You needn't worry, and Meg is the one buying a horse not me."

Graham sighed, "I am worried. As soon as you get near animals you lose all reason. If there is a poor creature there you will not be able to resist it." Confidently I said, "Well, I have said I'll go with her. I shall just have to prove you wrong."

The next morning Meg arrived and we set off for the market. The livestock pens were full of every imaginable type of horse. They came in all colours and sizes. They also came in all kinds of condition. I had never been to a horse sale before. I was saddened to see some of the poor creatures there. Some were elderly broken down horses, others were wild eyed and unbroken. Those horses in good condition and well schooled were easily sold and commanded good prices. The elderly wrecks were sold cheaply, to large men who loaded them unsympathetically, in groups onto horse lorries. I dared not think what was to become of them. Meg inspected the horses with her experienced eyes, but could not find one which suited her. The market was buzzing with people. In the crowds I recognised some familiar faces. One of these was a man called Tony, he worked for a local animal charity. It was a relief to see a friendly face and I went up to him and spoke, "Hello, what are you doing here?" Tony was a tall man, solidly built. His face was kindly, rosy cheeked, typical of people who spend all their lives working outside in all weathers.

He looked down at me and said, "I was just about to ask you the same question. I've come along to bid for a couple of the horses that need rescuing. The problem is there are too many here that need help. The charity can only help a few."

"I came with my friend, but she hasn't found any she likes. I shan't come to another horse sale; I didn't realise the sad cases I would see here. I hope you can save some of them. I had better go and join my friend. I may see you later." I said.

I wandered off, searching for Meg but I could not see her anywhere. Then the inevitable happened, I stopped by a pen, which contained three young colts. Each horse had a white sticker with a lot number glued to its back. In this group number 39 stood out for all the wrong reasons. His back bore the evidence of previous stickers, this poor creature had been trundled to horse sales before and it had taken its toll. He was a chestnut colt, with a white blaze and four white socks. He wore a head collar which was so tight it had begun to eat into his flesh. He stood totally dejected, his head held down and he had a discharge from his eyes and nose. I didn't know much about horses but I knew he would not make another sale day. The two other colts in the pen jostled around him. All his energy was deployed keeping himself upright.

My heart went out to him. I knew I would not be able to abandon him to fate. While I stood studying the pathetic creature, I heard a familiar voice." I've been looking for you. I have met a breeder of horses and I think he has got just the right horse for me. I have arranged to visit him next week and have a look. If you want to go home now, that's alright by me." I looked at Meg and said, "Look at this poor colt, I'm going to bid for him."

Chapter 32 – Lot 39

Meg was horrified, "You can't do that Ann! The creature is obviously ill. If he doesn't die it will cost you a fortune in vet fees, not only that, what would Graham say?" Wearily I replied, "I know you are talking sense, but I can't turn my back on him. If Graham saw this he would feel the same way too."

Meg was concerned, "I feel responsible, I should never have asked you to come along, please leave him, you don't know what you are letting yourself in for."

With dogged determination I said, "I'm going to bid for him, with or without your help."

Chapter 33
The Auction

Meg knew my mind was made up, "Well if you are intent on making a mistake I'm not going to let you make anymore. People at these auctions can be unscrupulous, I know some of the tricks they use. While you are bidding I'll keep an eye on what is going on." I was glad Meg would help. We wended our way to the auction ring and waited for Lot 39 to enter. Eventually the tired little colt entered the ring. The auctioneer began. "Who will give me twenty pounds for this colt?" The ring was silent, Meg told me not to bid, but wait. The silence was deafening, when the auctioneer boomed, "Who will give me fifteen pounds?" Meg gave me a nod and I bid for him. From across the ring someone else bid twenty pounds, and so it went on I bid against the unseen person until we reached forty pounds. I was fast approaching my limit, when Meg furiously whispered in my ear, "The other bidder is the dealer, they are just raising the stakes, the auctioneer must be in it as well." I was furious, the auctioneer looked towards me expecting my next bid, but he was in for a shock! He asked "You are not going to lose the sale for the sake of five pounds are you?"

With my adrenalin flowing I said, "I'm not bidding anymore."

The auctioneer became nervous, "Just bid one more pound, I'm sure he will be yours."

With anger in my voice I said, "I bet you know he'll be mine. You have been accepting bids from the man who is selling him. You thought you could push the price up without me knowing." The

Chapter 33 - The Auction

people round the ring stood in amazement waiting to see what would happen next. The unseen bidder came forward. He was a scruffy, burly insolent man, he spoke aloud, "You can have him for forty pounds."

By now my dander was up. Confidently, I said, "If I buy him it is at the price I bid before you began cheating." The look on the man's face was frightening, his face was turning puce with anger. He yelled, "I wouldn't want you for a wife."

My reply was quick and to the point, "I wouldn't want you for a husband if you were the last man on earth, so you won't be disappointed." Before the man could reply the people around the ring broke into applause and shouted to the auctioneer to let me have the colt. With the risk of a riot they had little choice but to sell me the poor creature. Meg was stunned. As we walked away people patted us on the back delighted the pair had got their comeuppance.

I may have managed to buy the colt but I had no way of getting him home. I found Tony and asked if he could help. As usual he was in control, "Don't worry Ann, I'll drop him off at the farm on the way back to the sanctuary with the ones I have bought."

Gratefully, I said, "Thanks, how much do I owe you?"

Laughing he said, "Absolutely nothing, the side show you put on was priceless. You never know they may think twice before they try that trick again."

Meg and I returned to the farm, it would not be long before Tony arrived. As soon as we drew up Graham met us on the drive. "It's nice to see you have been watching out for us, have you missed me?" I asked.

Graham looked around nervously, "I can't believe you did it Ann." I was puzzled how could he possibly know what happened at the sale. "Did what?" I asked.

His voice full of relief, "Come home without any more livestock."

There was no point in lying Tony would be arriving any minute. Hurriedly I said, "Well I have bought a young colt, but I had to get someone to transport it, they should be here shortly."

Graham's face went a similar shade to that of the dealer I had argued with. "You said you wouldn't buy anything. Why didn't you stop her Meg?"

Life on the Funny Farm

Meg was flustered, "I tried to stop her, but you know what Ann is like, she was determined to save the animal. I told her he would probably die, and even if he didn't, the vet's fees would be enormous."

Graham spluttered, "You have managed to buy an old crock, which will cost us a fortune. Have you taken leave of your senses?" Before I could reply Tony drove in with the horsebox. He opened the back door and tried to coax the frail creature down the ramp. Tottering from side to side the colt at last stood on the drive. Graham stared in disbelief. His voice full of anger, he said, "Who could let an animal get like that? Ann, get him comfy in a stable while I phone the vet." I did as I was instructed. Meg and I slowly walked with the horse to the stable yard. As we walked, Meg asked, "How did you know Graham would calm down after he saw him?" Happily I replied, "That's easy because beneath all that bluster he is a big softie!"

Within a short while Shona arrived to examine the colt, a cursory glance was all she needed. "Ann, this animal is very sick, we might be able to save him but it will be a long haul, are you up to it? She asked. This was what I had expected, needless to say we would give it a go. Over the next few weeks the colt, who we named Peanuts, was cared for by me, Jenny and Liz. The lice in his coat were eradicated, he was treated for ringworm. The wounds from the head collar were bathed daily and soothing ointment was gently applied. Slowly we introduced him to a diet of good hay and a bodybuilding bucket feed. The undernourished animal had never been fortunate to receive a prepared meal, and was reluctant to eat the nutritious foodstuff. All the coaxing in the world would not persuade him to sample the equine fayre. The only treat that Peanuts ate with relish was a polo mint. Over the next few weeks I bought out the supply of mints from the local shop and crushed them into his feed. His addiction to mints meant he would forage in the bucket trying to find the sweets, as he searched he could not avoid eating some of the prepared food. It was a long time before Peanuts would eat his rations without them being laced with polo's.   Each day we administered the antibiotics, and very slowly his strength returned. Within a couple of months Peanuts became an extremely pretty pony. His Chestnut coat glowed deep bronze, and his socks were darling white. His appearance was matched by his sparkling personality, his eyes twinkled with mischief,

Chapter 33 – The Auction

as he pranced around the field head held high. The transformation was complete, we had been rewarded in full for all our hard work.

Chapter 34
The Royal Show

Our wedding anniversary was approaching. Graham was busy training a manager for his London depot but he decided to return home during the week so we could celebrate. It would also test the potential manager's ability to run the business in Graham's absence. We decided to spend the day at The Royal Show and finish the day in style at a local restaurant. I was determined during the visit I would steer my husband towards the cattle sheds. This, I achieved easily. We walked along the lines looking at the various cattle breeds. At last we came to a row of the Scottish shaggy beasts. As usual my strategy was well rehearsed. "Look Graham, these are the cattle I told you about, aren't they impressive?" I asked.

Graham glanced at them indifferently, "They look all right, but we aren't having one," he flatly stated. I was not going to be deterred. I said, "You really like our home produced pork, just think how good our own beef would be. You love steak but it is so expensive, if we had our own supply you could eat it till the cows come home!"

Graham was unimpressed, "I think it is a lot easier just to buy meat from a butcher, we've got enough animals. Forget it Ann, you know nothing about cattle."

I was quite used to Graham's reluctance, but I persevered, "There is no harm in talking to some of the owners now that we are here." My long suffering partner sighed with resignation as I engaged the breeders in conversation.

Chapter 33 – The Auction

All of the owners were only too pleased to talk about the cattle, and explain the attributes of the breed. I hoped we would find someone with a steer for sale. With this in mind I approached a lady from Wales.

I enquired, "Do you ever have any steers for sale? I would like to be able to produce our own meat."

The small middle-aged woman spoke in a broad Welsh accent, "We don't have any steers to sell. You ought to start how I did, I bought a cow in calf and bred my own."

I glanced at Graham, his face was drained of all colour, his voice trembled as he spoke, "Oh my God, don't give her any ideas like that!"

It was too late; I thought it was a wonderful idea. The lady told us there was going to be a sale in October. It was the first sale to be held outside Scotland. It was ideal for us, as it was only fifty miles from our home. It was an opportunity we could not miss. I took all the details, I had just over two months to research cattle, in particular Highlanders.

Chapter 35
Intruders

We left the show in the late afternoon. As we drove home I chatted away enthusiastically about the prospect of owning our own cattle. Graham showed no such interest, hardly speaking at all. Once we were home we began to get ready for our candlelit anniversary meal. Graham was installed in the bathroom when Zac began to bark excitedly. Dogs are not unlike babies, in the respect they have a different kind of bark to fit the situation. A mother instinctively knows the reason her baby is crying. I was no different with Zac, that bark meant only one thing, intruders were on the farm. I peered out of the bedroom window. In the distance I could see people crouched down in the long grass by the top gate. I went downstairs, picked up Zac's training lead, this was his signal that he was on duty. We went into the compound and I opened the gate and walked towards the top entrance with my protector. As we approached I could see at least two people. By the gate was parked a camper van. I shouted, "This is private property, I'm letting my dog loose." With that I commanded Zac to chase the intruders. Two teenagers leapt out from the cover of the grass, vaulted over the gate and jumped into the waiting van. Zac was running at full speed, getting nearer to the gate, when a woman stood up trying valiantly to pull up her knickers. It was then I realised the group had stopped off to relieve themselves in the privacy of our garden. The woman continued to wrestle with her pants but Zac was getting closer by the second. Finally, the woman managed to reach the gate, her knickers still adrift. As the wo-

Chapter 35 - Intruders

man struggled to climb over the gate Zac homed in on her ample bare bottom. This gave her added impetus, with one final leap she reached the safety of the camper van. Once inside, the van sped off, leaving Zac staring down the lane, panting, his mouth wide open. If I had not known better I would have said he was grinning from ear to ear! I told Zac how clever he was and we returned to the house. I chuckled as I related the story to Graham, I don't think I shall ever forget the sight of that woman's bare backside scrambling over my gate!

The farm is very close to the City of Birmingham, and during the weekends many city dwellers walk along the lanes. The majority presented no problems, but there were others who have little or no understanding of livestock. During the summer I was busy mucking out the stables when I heard a tremendous commotion. My birds were clucking noisily. I stopped what I was doing and went to investigate. As soon as I had left the yard I could see what the trouble was. A large mongrel dog was running amok through my hens. Chantey had gone to the rescue of his women but the dog was not deterred by this fearsome rooster. I grabbed a broom and set off in pursuit, the dog may not have feared Chantey but a strange woman wielding a large yard brush was a different matter altogether. The mongrel ran to the gate, a lad stood there, clearly the thoughtless owner. I marched over to them and without further ado explained, "You do not let dogs off a lead around livestock. For good measure, I told the boy his stupidity may well have cost the lives of my birds. Once the boy had left with a well-deserved flea in his ear I went to find Chantey. The hens were all unscathed as Chantey had protected his harem, but I could not find my trusty cockerel anywhere. After much searching I found him behind a water butt, trembling and gasping for air. Gently I picked him up, examined him for any wounds but there were none. He was in shock and I knew enough to know that birds, when frightened can easily die of heart failure. I feared the worst, but as the day wore on his breathing returned to normal and he snuggled up with his hens for the night. I was relieved. We got away with it, but it was not the case. Over the next few days Chantey seemed to age before my eyes. He walked around slowly. No longer proudly strutting his stuff. He lost all interest in his women, he moped around the lawn. There was nothing I could do but take him to the vet.   Neville was a good vet but he would be the first to admit he knew little about birds. I walked into the consulting room and said, "I don't know what is wrong with Chantey. A dog attacked him a few days ago. Since then he has become like a little old man. He seems to have no energy, he is no longer interested in his girls. In fact, sex is completely off the menu. Is there anything you can suggest?"

Neville smiled wistfully, "Ann, if I knew the cure for that I would be a wealthy man! All I can suggest is give him some vitamins, see if they do the trick." I took Chantey home and gave him a course of pick me ups. Gradually he returned to his former self and within weeks he was ruling the roost.

Chapter 36
Free Range Turkeys

The heady days of summer were drawing to a close. People began to think about the imminent arrival of Christmas, and I was no exception. Fred had been very impressed with the turkeys I had supplied for the firm the previous year, and was keen for me to repeat the venture. I was reluctant to do so; the whole enterprise had given me a taste of commercial farming to which I was not suited. I decided to consult my farming oracle, Bert, to see what ideas he might have. I asked his advice, and watched as we went through the usual routine. He tipped his cap forward, scratched his thinning hair vigorously as though searching for inspiration. At last he spoke, "Well, Anna, you could have another go but this time use an old fashioned breed." I was intrigued and asked him to tell me more. Bert obliged, "The main breed of turkey used to be known as Bronze. They went out of vogue because the black feather roots were left behind on the skin. The housewife of today didn't like the effect, and as a consequence the white birds we have now grew in popularity. A similar thing has happened with eggs, the only ones you can buy in the shops now are brown; people no longer want a white egg."

I was intrigued, "What would the advantages of Bronze turkeys be for me? I asked.

Bert confidently replied, "They are very hardy, you could let them roam free on the farm, but like the hens you would have to confine them at night."

Life on the Funny Farm

I liked the sound of free-range turkeys, as usual Bert knew a man who reared them and within the week I was the proud owner of fifty burnished brown birds. Within a matter of days they were used to strutting around the garden and sitting in the lower branches of the oak trees surveying their world. I soon discovered that Turkeys did have personalities, two birds in particular caught my attention. Each day the hen and stag would sit and watch my house cleaning antics through my French window. As the work progressed they would tilt their heads from side to side absorbing all the different sounds. It gave the impression of oversized budgerigars. I knew the golden rule by heart – never give an animal a name if you are going to eat it, but this pair followed me everywhere. They were so absorbed in each other's company. I could not resist calling them Scarlett and Rhett. My plans for their demise had gone with the wind! Needless to say, I kept my thoughts to myself. Graham would find out soon enough!

Chapter 37
The Smiling Somali

September arrived, the last days of warmth would soon disappear. Before the weather turned unkind Meg and I travelled to Scotland for a cat show. We decided to make a weekend of it and Graham gallantly agreed to look after the farm and children.

Our hotel stay was enjoyable, but our visit to the show was going to be very significant. Whilst at the show I walked along the rows of cats. Every imaginable breed was represented, all were groomed to perfection, and then I caught sight of a breed I had never seen before. Sitting in a pen, looking serene was a grey, semi long-haired cat. To describe the cat as grey does not do justice to the intricate coat pattern. Around the golden eyes were what appeared to be carefully applied dark Eyeliner. The soft grey coat was enhanced by a warm mushroom undercoat. I studied the cat carefully, in return she gazed kindly at me, I knew then that what ever this cat was, I had to have one. I spent most of the day by her pen waiting for the owner to return. I had consulted my catalogue and I had discovered the cat was a Somali.

By mid afternoon the owner returned, I bombarded her with a list of questions; would a Somali live happily with a Burmese, were they good with children, and dogs, and because I was so busy did the long coat take a lot of grooming? The lady answered all my questions, as she spoke I realised she was a kindred spirit. She too ran a small holding, owned Burmese and had a family. Her Somalis fitted in well, their coats didn't knot so the grooming was not a time consuming occupation. Her enthusiasm made me all the more determined to acquire one of them. Finding a Somali kitten was not going to be an easy task. There were very few of them in the country, as they had been imported a couple of years earlier. Unlike Burmese they did not produce large litters. In fact, often they gave birth to only one kitten at a time. If I really wanted one I should have to be patient. I have always believed anything worth having, is worth waiting for. I decided to contact the small group of breeders in Britain, in the hope that one of them may be able to find me a suitable kitten. The weekend sped by, I could not wait to get home and tell Graham all about the new breed of cat I had seen. Graham did not share my enthusiasm, he said, "Ann, don't you think we have enough cats?"

Unperturbed I replied, "One more cat won't make a difference, it would give me a new challenge to learn about different pedigrees."

Sternly, Graham met my gaze, "The problem is, it won't stop at one cat, this place is beginning to resemble Noah's Ark, all the animals come in pairs, and then they multiply."

Crossly I said, "You needn't worry about umpteen Somalis, they are very difficult to come by, it will take me months to find a suitable kitten, let alone more than one."

Graham let out a prolonged sigh, "It doesn't really matter what I say. You will still go and do exactly what you want anyway. Just don't expect me to get enthusiastic about more cats." I saw no point in continuing the conversation. One day, I was sure I would have a Somali. Until then, I had other things to occupy my mind.

September was drawing to a close; the cattery and kennels would soon be quieter as the holiday season ended. The busy stream of customers arriving with their pets would cease; the constant telephone enquiries would soon become spasmodic. During the quiet months we would busy ourselves preparing the buildings for the next hectic round of holidays. The lull in business gave me time to find out all I could about Highland Cattle; the sale was fast approaching. I joined The Highland Cattle Society, and began studying cattle pedigrees. When I wasn't engrossed in bovine books I was hot on the trail of a Somali kitten. The search for a new feline was proving difficult; none seemed to be available and I knew I would have to be patient.

Joe and Lucy found September a momentous month as they began life at the local junior school. Graham was still working in London.

Chapter 37 – The Smiling Somali

His manager had settled in well but my husband was reluctant to release the reigns of his new venture. Matters came to a head early one Saturday morning. The children delighted in their father's return at the weekend; they would rush into our bedroom, bounce happily on the bed and spend an hour relating their adventures to Graham. This Saturday was no different; the three of them chatted away contentedly. Joe sat on the bed, his little legs tucked under his body. Staring earnestly at his father he asked, "When are you going to be a proper Daddy again?" The room fell silent, Graham did not need to ask what his young son meant. My husband was quick to reply, "I think you are right, it's time I left other people to run the depot in London. I shall still have to go for the odd day but from now on I shall stay in Birmingham." The children had their father full time again, and I had my mate home, who I thought would be very supportive when the cattle arrived!

Chapter 38
Sale Day

At long last the day of the cattle sale arrived. Joe and Lucy were packed off to school and Liz agreed to look after them if we had not returned by the end of the school day. Graham and I set off with the livestock trailer hitched to the back of the car. En route we collected Meg. I would need her farming expertise when viewing the cattle. Her father was a cattle farmer and she had grown up knowing the finer points of these creatures. It was a damp bitterly cold day when we departed. Meg and I were well wrapped up in our wax coats. Our willies were lined with three pairs of socks; from past experience we knew the auction ring would be cold. Neither of us would have won a fashion parade but we were on a mission. Underneath all my layers of clothes a money bag was tightly strapped to my waist. Inside was one thousand pounds which I had scraped together to purchase my dream cow. I had no more money; this was my limit. I wondered if it would be enough.

The journey only lasted an hour; Graham parked the trailer in a side street, away from the market. Puzzled, I asked, "Why don't you park in the market?"

His business acumen shone through as he said, "If they see we have got a trailer they will know we intend to buy something. You know what these auctions can be like, they will push the price up." I remembered vividly how I had been duped when I bought Peanuts, I did not want to repeat the experience. Once in the market we spent time looking at all the cattle. I had decided I would buy a cow in calf,

Chapter 38 – Sale Day

there were only three likely candidates. The first was a yellow female, in calf. She was beautifully turned out, I knew instinctively she was a class act. The other two were red cows, both were in calf and both had a calf at foot. Any of these three would do me nicely. Meg agreed that there did not seem to be anything amiss with them.

The three of us entered the sale ring and found a space on the benches which surrounded the sawdust-covered arena. As we waited for the sale to begin we chatted to the people around us. They were all friendly and wanted to know which lots we were interested in. Meg whispered, "Don't tell them in too much, they'll soon find out which ones have caught your interest." I heeded Meg's words and was non-committal. The first beasts to enter the ring were the heifers, for the uninitiated, these are females, which have not yet been bred from. I watched fascinated, as they were put through their paces. The auctioneer who was an elderly man began the bidding, the price climbed quickly and soon it was well past my budget. This happened time and time again. I was deflated as I spoke to Meg, "I can't afford these, if the youngsters are fetching these prices I may as well go home now." Meg turned towards me and said, "We've come this far let's wait and see. If you don't get one today there will be other chances." I did not share her optimism, I had set my heart on one of these shaggy beasts

The sale dragged on, there was no reduction in the prices. If anything the buyers were getting more enthusiastic, and spending more money. At last the beautiful yellow cow came into the ring. Meg forcefully said, "Don't bid straight away. Wait until there is a lull in the bidding then strike." Megs words were not needed, it seemed everyone there wanted the cow, the bidding rapidly approached three thousand guineas, and I hadn't raised my catalogue once! The next lot entered the ring, one of the two red cows in calf with a calf at foot. The auctioneer raised his voice, "Who will give me a thousand guineas for this lot, don't forget you are buying three lives."

Somewhere a bid of five hundred rang out. Slowly the bidding reached eight hundred. The enthusiasm of the buyers seemed to have waned. Tentatively, I raised my catalogue. At long last, I was bidding for a Highland cow. By the time we reached nine hundred it was between a gentleman and me; the rest had withdrawn. My heart began to race, I perched on the edge of the bench. At last I reached my limit of one thousand. The auctioneer cajoled the other bidder to good effect wrestling another hundred guineas from his grasp. Graham had sat silently throughout, but now he touched my arm and said, "Go on bid again I'll lend you the extra money." For a moment I was sorely tempted but I refused, I knew my limit and I had reached it. The auctioneer stared in my direction and asked, "Any more bids?" I shook my head and settled back on the bench, close to tears.

The third and final cow entered the ring with her red steer at foot. Her belly was enormous announcing to the world the new life growing inside. She had huge handle bar horns, a long shaggy fringe from which peeked out large liquid eyes framed with huge eyelashes. She looked grand and had a name to match, she was Viscountess of the Brand. Her owner walked her round the ring as the auctioneer opened the bidding. "Who will give me a thousand for this beautiful beast?" Just as before, the buyers seemed to have lost their enthusiasm, or perhaps they had spent all their money. The bidding was slow. Once again at eight hundred guineas I raised my catalogue. The price slowly crept upwards, my limit getting closer all the time. I bid nine hundred and eighty and waited for my hopes to be dashed again. The auctioneer scanned the room searching for bids that refused to come, he shouted, "Will any one give me twenty guineas more?" The ring was silent, his voice boomed, "She's going to the gate, I shall sell her, any more offers?" My heart was pounding in my ribs, I sat on the edge of my seat gasping for breaths of air as my body had a rush of adrenalin.

Still the auctioneer scanned the room for more bids at last he turned to the owner and gave him a questioning look, the owner gave a slight nod of his head. The auctioneer spoke, "I'm selling this cow for nine hundred and eighty guineas. This is your last chance." By now I was drumming the catalogue fiercely against my leg, wishing he would lower the hammer, everyone around us could not mistake my excitement. The room remained silent. At last, I heard the words I had dreamt of, "Sold to the lady on my right." Relief flooded through my veins, the strangers who surrounded us had been caught up with my infectious desire, and a round of applause broke out spontaneously from the benches.

The three of us scrabbled out of our seats and hurried to the stalls to meet my new acquisition.

Chapter 39
Tess Comes Home

The cow had returned to a stall and her owner stood with her. The man was in his fifties, he clearly cared for his stock and began to tell me all about her.

"You have bought a good cow." He began, "We call her Tess, her calf answers to the name Sam. She is halter trained, she has no vices, her next calf is due April. Take good care of her. She's ten years old now but she should go on for another ten years if you are lucky." Graham collected the trailer, and with the help of the vendor we loaded her and the calf. As soon as we arrived home we walked the beasts to a stable, fed and watered them and left them to settle in their new home. I often look back fondly on that day, it truly was one of the best days ofn my life. In the future I would purchase more cattle from sales but none would be as exhilarating as the first time. The arrival of Tess and Sam caused quite a stir in the village. These Scottish cattle were a novelty, not least amongst the farming fraternity. Bert, who had known of my plans was the first to acquaint himself with the hairy beasts. He was a man who was used to the continental breeds, and in the beginning they held little allure for him. But as the years have rolled by, he too has become a proud owner of this hardy breed. It became commonplace to see cars drawing up, their occupants climbing out and peering over the field gate to stare at a sight so familiar on picture post cards from Scotland. Tess and Sam loved all the attention. Both were good natured, they knew their names; it did not take them long to come running towards me when

Life on the Funny Farm

their names were called. I spent as much time as I could with them; come the Spring Tess would calve, and I needed to gain her trust.

The chill winds of winter had begun to bite. Most of the animals spent their time inside sheltering from the forbidding climate. Not so the cattle, they were purpose-built for the colder climate. They would stand majestically in the field, the wind rippling through their dense coats, enjoying every minute.

Chapter 40
The Man from Italy

Looking after the animals became harder as the ice created a slippery surface, and the water taps froze into submission. Few people ventured to take a holiday, but we had a small group of pets staying whose owners sought the warmth of other lands. One such pet was a trusting golden Labrador. Her owner was Italian, Mr. Ricardo. He regularly visited his home country of Italy and entrusted us with the care of his beloved dog. The first time I met Mr. Ricardo I was struck by his resemblance to Marlon Brando's portrayal of the Godfather. He was dressed in a suit befitting any Mafia boss, around his neck he wore a heavy duty gold chain. Around his wrists he sported a Rolex watch and multiple chunky gold bracelets. From the Panama hat on his head, to the two-tone leather shoes on his feet he was dressed for the part. Each time he visited Italy it was for a period of a month. Sometimes, this would be extended due to personal reasons.

Each time he collected his dog, Lisa, he would pay cash. From his pocket he would pull out a wad of money and peel off a few notes. He was clearly a wealthy man, but he loved his canine companion dearly. Lisa wanted for nothing. Her favourite past time was playing with a football. If the England football team could dribble a ball as well as her we would win the World Cup every time. To make sure Lisa would continue her foot balling skills whilst she was kennelled he brought along her football. This wasn't any old ball; it was top of the range leather signed by the Italian football team! My son Joe was very envious of Lisa's toy.

Lisa was a regular visitor, it is unusual to learn much information about our customers. Our clients come from all walks of life, doctors, teachers, factory workers but they all share a common interest – the love of their pet. I used to joke with Graham that Mr. Ricardo was a member of the Mafia, there is a saying, 'Many a true word spoken in jest!' I don't know the truth of the matter but I did begin to wonder. Just before Lisa was due to be collected Marco, the owner's son, rang to say his father had been delayed in Italy as he had a funeral to attend. This wasn't the first time someone had passed away while Mr. Ricardo was visiting his native country. It did not present us with a problem as Lisa could stay as long as was necessary. Marco arrived at the farm some days later to give us some money on account. We chatted happily. Marco informed me, "My father has an estate in Italy but he will not return permanently while he has Lisa in case she is upset by the upheaval." I knew Mr. Ricardo was besotted with his dog, and was not surprised at this news. It was some weeks later when Marco returned to collect Lisa; his father had returned. Marco began hurriedly searching through his pockets, panic began to rise as he realised he had forgotten his wallet. By now he had broken into a cold sweat, with hands trembling he asked, "Can I take Lisa, I will return with the money, but if she is not in the house when my father returns he will be furious with me." There was no mistaking the fear in the man's eyes. This was a regular customer; I thought it highly unlikely I would not receive my money so I agreed to let him take the dog. The days passed by but there was no sign of my money. At last, I wrote to Mr. Ricardo requesting the bill be settled. The next day the phone rang; the voice was unmistakably that of Mr Ricardo. He spoke with a strong Italian accent. "What is this about a not having been paid for my Lisa?" I explained what had happened. The voice at the other end of the phone was chillingly cold, "I gave my son the money. I know what he has done he has spent it on something else, I will kill him! You look after my Lisa so well, if he has upset you I will deal with him." I remembered the fear shown by Marco and tried to make light of the situation, but Mr. Ricardo was having none of it. Later that day Marco arrived very shamefaced

Chapter 40 – The Man From Italy

with the money. I said I was sorry I had contacted his father but there was little else I could do. Marco was apologetic and hoped it would not affect Lisa staying with us in the future. I assured him it would not. As he was leaving, he said, "You don't understand, my father is not a man to cross." After my unnerving phone conversation with Mr. Ricardo I shared his son's misgivings, I just hoped that nothing would ever happen to Lisa whilst she was in my care.

Chapter 41
Christmas Shopping

Just as I knew little about my customers, they in turn only saw me on the farm. They were quite used to me greeting them in my burgundy uniform. All the staff wear a uniform, which apart from saving their clothes gives an air of professionalism. Christmas was fast approaching, I decided to be organised and shop for presents in the local town. The trip was progressing well; I decided to buy a nightie for my mother-in-law, Rose. I went into the local branch of Marks and Spencers, and soon found something suitable. As I was making my way to the pay point I bumped in to an elderly lady who had boarded her cats with me almost from the moment we had opened. She was clearly pleased to see me as she said, "Fancy seeing you here. Are you doing your Christmas shopping?" I replied in the affirmative, and we continued to chat.

Her husband stood beside her, and it was clear, that although he knew me, he could not recollect from where he knew me. The puzzlement showed on his face as he valiantly tried to remember who I was. I asked, "How are Topsy and Honey, are they still as affectionate as ever?" Suddenly, the penny had dropped a smile of recognition crossed his face. Excitedly he shouted, "I didn't recognise you with your clothes on!" The ladies lingerie department fell silent, all eyes turning in my direction, then furtive glances towards the contents of my basket. In an equally loud voice I replied "When you are used to seeing someone in uniform it is difficult to recognise them in normal

Chapter 40 – The Man From Italy

dress." I glanced around but the look on the faces of those around me conveyed their disbelief at my explanation. With my reputation in tatters I hurriedly paid for my goods and beat a hasty retreat!

Christmas was drawing ever closer. The turkeys were growing rapidly, and would make fine festive dinners. As the Yuletide season approached I worried constantly that the birds might be subject to the attentions of rustlers. There were a number of farms in the locality which reared poultry for the Christmas trade. The local police force made their presence felt in the area to deter would-be thieves. However, they could not deter the four legged, cunning hunter, the fox. Our pens were secure at night. Occasionally, over the years the odd hen would not return to the coop, and the fox always managed to get an easy take-away. I accepted this as part of country life, but in early December I was paid a visit by my local fox, which left me sickened.

Chapter 42
Brer Fox Does His Worst

As usual I awoke early. As soon as it was light I went to let the birds out for the day. As I walked across the lawn I saw a small heap lying on the grass. I went to investigate, to my horror it was the remains of one of my hens. Some yards away lay another bundle of feathers. I scanned the garden realising the corpses lay everywhere. In all, over a dozen of my hens had been slaughtered. The marauding fox had only eaten a couple of them, the rest had been decapitated, and cast aside in his killing spree. I rushed to the coop to discover the fox had ripped away the bottom panels to gain entry. Inside, the remaining birds sat huddled together in shock. The saddest blow was the discovery of Chantey's body by the door. He had died trying to protect his ladies from the onslaught.

When I was a child my father, Tom, had kept hens and he had experienced the attentions of foxes, so I knew they were a threat to poultry. But until this moment I did not realise their true capabilities. The urban fox is growing in numbers all the time, partly due to the fact that people encourage them by providing food. The cubs may look endearing but they grow into wasteful, killing machines. If people realised the wicked devastation they caused I doubt they would be so keen to help their numbers increase.

Poultry are not their only tasty titbit; newborn lambs are easy prey for this wily customer. Over the years I have encountered many foxes, they are bold and show no fear. Having held their sadistic party they returned a few nights later, this time my geese were on the menu. For-

Chapter 40 – The Man From Italy

tunately Zac woke me from my slumbers with his persistent barking. I rushed out of bed, turned the floodlights on, and saw a group of three foxes attacking my geese. The gander, Laddie, was doing his best to fend off the attack and save his women, but the hunters had the upper hand. I rushed outside, grabbing a yard broom as I ran. The foxes glanced in my direction unconcerned. I beat them away with the broom, but they would not give up, instead they stood a short distance away ready to attack again. I called to my trusty guard for assistance. Zac came running at full speed, and the cowardly foxes retreated. My geese were battered and bruised but thankfully they lived to tell the tale. The foxes continued to be a major problem for the next couple of months, but I managed to thwart their efforts. Eventually the matter was solved in the only way possible. The neighbouring farmer had begun lambing, in one week alone six new born lambs were murdered by the foxes. My neighbour tied a chicken carcass near to his house, sure enough the marauders came, and from the comfort of his bedroom he took aim with his shotgun. The solution was inevitable, but once again the poultry were safe, and no more ewes would grieve for their lambs, which they could not protect.

Christmas came and went. The roast bronze turkey was a great success. The family enjoyed the succulent meat. As we ate, Rhett and Scarlett peered in through the French window watching the festivities. Graham was reluctant to spare them, until I pointed out that we could rear our own turkey poults in the Spring. At the time I really believed that it would be possible, but I had no idea what a full grown stag turkey was capable of!

Chapter 43
Sonasag Arrives

The New Year arrived, the cattle had settled on the farm well. We had heard of a dispersal sale of Highland cattle due to take place at a farm in Oxford. I had the opportunity to view the beasts before the auction, so Liz and I visited the farm. It was a huge, well-run farm, with every conceivable piece of equipment. The cattle were all kept meticulously, and with the exception of one, were superb examples of the breed.

The manager of the Fold met us. The collective name for a group of Highland cattle is not a herd but they are referred to as a fold. This is because in their native Scotland they were housed in enclosures called folds. The manager had reached retiring age, what he didn't know about Highland cattle you could write on a postage stamp.

The time sped by as he showed us around and introduced us to the cows. There were at least seven cows which I would have been proud to own. Just before we left he showed us one more cow.

She was very different from the others; she was yellow in colour, but her horns turned inwards spoiling the effect that is characteristic of the breed. I was unimpressed, she had a miserable look on her face, her belly was huge, only in part due to the calf she was carrying. She was old and her muscle tone had long since vanished. Imagine my surprise when the manager who was called Bill, made a great fuss of her, clearly she was a favourite. Bill couldn't wait to tell us about her. "This cow is seventeen years old, she is not a full Highland. She is part longhorn that is why her horns are shaped differently. She's due

Chapter 43 – Sonasag Arrives

to calve next month, she usually has heifer calves. Her name is Sonasag." It is the custom to give Highland beasts Gaellic names, hers meant happy little cow. Looking at her I felt nothing could have been less apt. I was certain about one thing, we would try and buy one of the cows offered for sale, but Sonasag wouldn't be one of them.

The following week Graham, Meg and I set off for the sale. Once again I had managed to save my pennies, which were tightly strapped to my body in my trusty moneybag. The sale took place on the farm; after the beasts were sold the machinery would be auctioned. There was a good turn out of people, once again many had endless supplies of money to spend. One man in particular had money to burn, every cow I wanted to purchase so did he. Each time he outbid me effortlessly. At the end of the day, I calculated he had spent over forty thousand pounds buying a handful of beasts. Unlike my first sale, I was not desperate to buy a cow. I could wait for another opportunity. All the good cows were sold. I had just suggested to Graham that we leave, when the old cow Sonasag ambled into the ring. Graham said, "Why don't you bid for her?" I gave him a withering look as I replied, "She is as old as the hills, and she doesn't even look like a Highlander. If I take that home I shall be a laughing stock with the other farmers." Meg had been silent up to now but she spoke with authority, "You might have a bargain here. She is carrying a calf, if it is a heifer it will be worth something. She is worth about two hundred and fifty pounds for meat, if you bid that you can't lose. My father certainly wouldn't laugh at a deal like that."

I listened to what she said, and could see the sense of it but the cow in front of me did not fit my majestic view of the breed. Reluctantly I decided to bid for her. The other people were as unimpressed as I was, the auctioneer asked for two hundred and fifty pounds but no one responded. Eventually a bid of one hundred and fifty was offered. Half-heartedly, I raised my hand and with no opposition Sonasag was sold to me for two hundred pounds. There was no heady excitement as I walked to the office to pay for her. Graham went to collect her from the cattle shed, and within minutes I joined him. "Haven't you found anyone to load her?" I asked.

Graham said, "Yes, but the man said this was the Boss's cow and he would want to say farewell to her, he's gone to fetch him." We stood there a while longer, then I saw someone I had met at the previous sale. I walked away to chat to them. In the meantime, Bill the manager had arrived at our trailer with Sonasag. I returned just in time to hear Bill ask, "Is it you who bought the old girl?"

Graham replied, "No, it was my wife, here she is now."

Bill turned around and saw me, his face broke into a relieved smile as he said, "Oh, I'm so glad you bought her, I know you will be kind to her, she will reward you."

Bill loaded the old cow into the livestock carrier, it was clear to see he was quite upset to see her go. It was not until a week later when I received a letter with her pedigree that I realised Bill was her owner. Inside the letter was a five-pound note, good luck money. Bill wrote that he hoped she would give me a heifer; well, I would not have long to wait.

When we returned home we bedded the cow down in a stable for the night. It was quite clear she was unimpressed with her new home. She had come from a modern, all-conveniences home to a farm which would not have been out of place in the nineteen fifties. The first shock she had was her water bucket. Until now, she had been used to an automatic water supply system. The look on her face when she put her nose in the bucket was one of utter disdain. The next morning I turned her out into the field where she met Tess and Sam. The fact there were other Highlanders here made the situation bearable. However, she moped around the field. When I called she chose to ignore me. It took a number of weeks before she would acknowledge my existence. I began to wonder if she would ever forget her beloved Bill. It is documented that cattle remember their stockman for three years, I hoped Sonasag would make do with a stockwoman sooner, rather than later. Gradually she made the best of a bad job and settled down to life on the farm.

Chapter 44
A Calf is Born

Signs of spring were evident; the daffodils were sporting tightly closed flowers, and my two pregnant cows were nearing their confinement. I spent my spare moments terrifying myself reading about problem calvings. I wasn't sure I was cut out for this. My breed manual warned me that whilst Highland Cattle were a docile breed, when a cow had a newborn calf at foot they could become very protective and aggressive. My confidence was not improved when Bert paid me a visit. He arrived waving a farming publication. Agitatedly, he thrust it under my nose, "You had better read this Anna. There was a woman up in Yorkshire, like you she had a few Highlanders. One of them calved, she was so excited she rushed in to see the baby. The cow took exception to sharing her babe and attacked the woman. The horn penetrated the brain and killed her." Sure enough the article recounted all the gory details. I began to wonder if I had bitten off more than I could chew.

A few days later Sonasag began to spurn the company of Tess and Sam. She spent most of her time in the corner of the field. I knew the birth was imminent. I had hoped she would settle in the shelter, but she had chosen the place for her delivery and nothing would persuade her otherwise. I didn't witness the birth. Cows like their privacy, she waited until I went out shopping before she gave birth effortlessly to a bonny heifer calf. With great care I visited the new arrival. Sonasag gave me a baleful stare but allowed me to inspect her babe. With low gentle mooing she talked to her calf. This large beast cleaned and nurtured her offspring with such gentleness. I felt privileged to be allowed to observe it. Within an hour the calf was able to stand. It took its first tentative steps, staying close to its mother. When the calf had dried it resembled a huge teddy bear and to this day I don't think any calf is as appealing as one of my Scottish refugees.

The day drew to an end. I had my first calf, all had gone well. Graham and I finally retired to bed, relieved the day was over. As we lay in bed waiting for sleep to come the rain began to lash against the windows. The wind howled as a storm set in. I could not sleep, my thoughts were with the new born calf being subjected to the elements. As I continued to toss and turn Graham irritably asked, "What's the matter with you?"

"I can't help worrying about that calf out in this weather." I replied.

Graham sat up, "For goodness sake the cow will have taken her in the shelter, go to sleep." With that, he rolled over.

Graham was probably right, but there was nothing else for it but to go and check the calf was safe. I climbed out of bed and began to dress.

Graham asked, "What are you doing now?"

As I pulled a thick jumper over my head I replied, "I'm going to the field to make sure everything is alright."

"You are completely mad. You're not going out there alone, I'll come with you."

With that Graham began to dress, he put a jersey and trousers over his pyjamas, and together we donned our waterproofs, and wellies. Armed with a powerful torch we battled through the storm to the field. One glance in the shelter confirmed my worst fears, it was empty. Somewhere out in the paddock was the mother and calf, being buffeted by the wind and rain. The powerful beam of the torch shone over the ground, finally picking out the form of Sonasag. Nestled by her back leg, lay the wet bedraggled babe. We could not leave them to the mercy of the weather, we called and called but she would not budge. Graham was getting impatient he said,

"There is nothing else for it. I'm not spending all night out here. I'll pick the calf up and bring it into the shelter." Quickly I said, "I don't think that is a good idea, she might attack you."

Chapter 44 – A Calf is Born

Graham would not be deterred, we walked towards the pair, Graham hoisted the calf in to his arms and slowly walked towards the shelter. Sonasag followed closely behind, not once did she threaten us. We settled the couple into a warm dry straw bed and returned to the comfort of our bed. I lay for a short while thinking about the events of the day. I was truly concerned that the cow might have attacked us. If my husband had been gored to death in the field, whilst wearing his pyjamas, I was sure no jury in the land would have believed my story!

Chapter 45
Turkey Trot

Spring had truly arrived; the daffodils were in full bloom. In the field both cows had their new babies beside them. Tess had followed the example of Sonasag, and had waited for me to leave the farm before she gave birth to a bull calf. I named the calves, the heifer was called Sunny and the male was given the apt name of Oxo. They delighted in each other's company. Their mothers kept a watchful eye on their exuberant play. Sam slid into the role of big uncle with ease; all was a picture of contentment in the field. As usual, springtime stirred the sexual desires of almost all the animals on the farm. The gander, Laddie, had made a complete recovery from his entanglement with the fox, and turned his amorous attentions to his lady friends. Anthony spent every spare moment courting Cleopatra but the most macho of all was Rhett, the turkey stag. Not content with smothering Scarlet with his basic desires, he began to harass the hens.

Their lives had not been complete since the demise of Chantey, there was only one solution to find them a new rooster. Meg came to the rescue with an adolescent cockerel which was surplus to her father's requirements. Maybe because he was young, he had a belligerent air; he was so sure of himself. It was not hard to think of a name for him. Cocky by name and cocky by nature. It took him no time at all to realise what hens were for. Rhett was displeased by the arrival of this male upstart, but turned his attentions to another female. Rhett began a long love affair with my young kennel maid, Gemma.

Chapter 44 – A Calf is Born

In the beginning he would follow Gemma as she carried out her work, his attentions seemed harmless. As time progressed he would puff out his feathers, giving the appearance of a bird twice his size. When this did not attract her attention, he began his intricate courtship dance. Gemma was amused by his antics, often giving him a tasty morsel. At first, Rhett accepted the gifts graciously, but his attentions became more persistent. Until, finally he charged at Gemma in an effort to mate her. The more she spurned his affections the more persistent and aggressive he became. On numerous occasions I had to rescue her from a stable in which she had sought sanctuary. Rhett would stand outside in a threatening manner, waiting for his intended conquest. This ritual was carried out with greater intensity each day until we confined the pair of turkeys to their house until the mating season was over!

Chapter 46
The First Family Holiday

Life on the farm had provided Joe and Lucy with experiences that most people would never be able to share and as a consequence, their lives for most part had been enriched. There was one thing they had never experienced, a family holiday. We had taken short breaks, but Graham decided it was time we all had a real holiday. Our destination was Jersey. We planned to be away for eight days, Gemma and Liz moved into the house and were responsible for running the business in my absence.

We journeyed to Jersey on a ferry; we had booked into a hotel with full board. This was my idea of a holiday, no cleaning or cooking for a whole week. Within a couple of days, I was suffering withdrawal symptoms. Some people are addicted to alcohol, others to nicotine, but I couldn't be without animals. To satisfy my needs, each day we would visit an animal attraction. I had long been a fan of Gerald Durrell and had read his books avidly. We visited his zoo where he had done sterling work in trying to conserve endangered species. I have visited most zoos that exist in Britain. Some have filled me with dismay, but this one was very different. They had a good breeding record, this was evidence the animals were content, as only relaxed creatures will embark on reproduction. We visited a farm devoted to the magnificent Shire Horses. These huge, gentle beasts whose rippling muscles gave them a majestic air were testament to a bygone age. As the week wore on we were running out of animal attractions and in desperation I visited a farm, which owned a herd of the pretty

Chapter 46 – The First Family Holiday

doe eyed Jersey cattle. Joe and Lucy enjoyed their holiday, spending most of their time in the hotel swimming pool. They were well used to their mother's peculiar needs when it came to animals. They were now proper little people; no longer helplessly relying on us to tend for all their needs. Lucy was an extrovert. She would engage everyone she met in conversation. Joe was less confident, and appeared shy in comparison with his sister. Nevertheless, both had inherited a love of animals, and were compassionate in their handling of them. Towards the end of our stay we went to the dining room for lunch. The room looked out over a flat roof, positioned in the centre was a far from happy seagull. You didn't need to be a qualified vet to realise the obscene angle of the wing bore witness to a broken bone. Lucy spied the bird, and became very agitated. "Mummy," she declared, "look at that poor bird, something will have to be done to help him." Before I could reply she climbed down from her chair and strode in a purposeful manner towards the restaurant manager. I watched as the tall man looked down on the small diminutive figure, he listened intently and assured Lucy they would help the bird. Like all children patience is a word they do not comprehend. Lucy was no different she demanded immediate action. The other diners watched amused as two waiters climbed precariously through the window, then walked apprehensively towards what was in fact, a large bird with an even larger beak! The mangled wing was a handicap, so much so, it surrendered gracefully and was brought to the safety of the dining room. The bird was taken to a local sanctuary where the wing was attended to. Before we left Jersey, at the insistence of Lucy, we visited the bird to make sure he was being well cared for. Lucy left the island content in the knowledge that the bird would make a full recovery.

Whilst I had enjoyed my holiday I could not wait to return to my beloved animals at home. The day of departure arrived, we said our farewells to the staff and other guests. The ferry was due to leave in the early evening so during the afternoon we visited a park where to my delight a brass band was giving a concert. I have been a fan of this kind of music for as long as I can remember. It may be attributed to the fact, that as a child, Tom and Emily had taken me to the seaside resort of Eastbourne. There, most early evenings we would sit and listen to the band playing. It remains a delightful childhood memory. The four of us sat whiling the time away before we could board the ferry, listening to the stirring marching tunes. I was happy; within twelve hours we would be home. We left the park and drove to the ferry. We were in good time but as we approached we were surprised there was so little activity. There were no cars queuing; perhaps we were too early. We got out of the car and stared out across the vast expanse of sea. In the distance was the ferry boat, not sailing into the harbour but away from it! Realisation was not slow to dawn, we had missed the boat!

My immediate reaction was one of disbelief. Graham strode to the office. Within minutes, he returned to the car. In a resigned voice he said, "Ann you are not going to like this, there is not another ferry until tomorrow morning. The good news is they have altered our tickets so we can sail on that boat."

My mind was racing; there was so much to do. I rang the farm to tell Liz and Gemma that we would not be returning as planned. They were none too happy either. During my absence there had been no problems, but where animals are concerned you can never tell when one will become ill or worse still try to carry out a suicide mission. The strain of the responsibility was beginning to tell on the staff. They had contented themselves with the knowledge I would be in charge by the morning. Now they had another day of worry to contend with. We rang the hotel we had left that morning. Fortunately, they had a vacant room so we returned to our holiday base. The journey to the Hotel was strained. Graham had been responsible for the ferry tickets, I had only glanced at them when we received them. The shock had subsided, now I wanted some answers. In a frosty tone I asked, "How could we have gotten the time wrong?" Graham was subdued as he replied, "I think I must have misread the time on the ticket, but it's not all my fault. You should have checked as well."

My anger was simmering away, "How could I look at the tickets? You wanted to keep them safe. I don't understand how you could get the time wrong, you needn't blame me for this one." I angrily declared.

Graham sighed; another frosty silence was about to descend, but not before he said, "The tickets said the boat left at sixteen hundred hours, I don't know why but I got it fixed in my brain that it was six o'clock."

Chapter 46 – The First Family Holiday

Curtly, I said, "For future reference get it fixed in your brain
six o'clock is eighteen hundred hours, and four o'clock is surprisingly sixteen hundred hours." The rest of the journey to the hotel was spent in a resentful silence. That evening, as we entered the dining room the other guests were amazed to see us. We were bombarded with questions, our predicament provided them with great amusement. With a good meal inside us, we too, in our usual fashion began to see the funny side and joined in with their merriment. The next morning we left for the ferry much earlier than we needed to, but there was no way I was going to miss that boat! A day later than planned, we arrived home. The saying 'There is no place like home' could not have been more apt. I made it quite clear to Graham that should we ever embark on a family holiday again, the tickets would be my responsibility!

Chapter 47
A Somali Take-Over

I felt refreshed after the holiday, the staff had looked after the farm and its residents well. The calves were thriving, Scarlett was sitting on a clutch of eggs, the cats and dogs were all fit and well. Life was good, but it was about to get even better, for me at least. We had been home for less than a week when one Sunday evening the phone rang. I answered it and a woman's voice enquired, "Are you still looking for a Somali?" My heart skipped a beat, my search so far for this new breed of cat had been fruitless. I quickly replied, "Yes, I am but no one seems to have a blue female kitten."

The woman replied, "I don't have a kitten but I do have an adult blue female available." My heart sank, the breed was still very rare in the UK and no one in their right mind would part with an adult unless there was something wrong with it. I asked, "Why are you selling her?"

The woman replied, "I am going to emigrate, I not only breed Somalis but I also own Maine Coons, Burmese, and Abyssinians. I have decided not to take the Somalis with me." At least her explanation helped to allay my fears. I arranged to visit her home the next day and meet her cats. I knew that when presented with a number of cats my enthusiasm might run away with me, so I took Liz along to curb my impetuosity.

The lady who was called Sue did not live far away, within an hour of travelling we had reached her tidy, modern town house. Inside, the array of cats which greeted us was amazing. Each room was occupied by felines; young kittens strolled about without a care in the world.

Chapter 47 – A Somali Take-Over

In all, Sue had over forty adult cats of which only half were emigrating with her. One of the first cats to welcome us was the object of my visit, a beautiful blue Somali called Tibby. It was love at first sight for both of us, there was no question we were made for each other. Sue showed me her other females, Beattie, a delicate fawn girl and April a striking sorrel silver, one of the first of that colour to be bred in this country. It would have been so easy to take them all but my finances would not allow it. I could only afford one of these beautiful, sociable cats.

I was curious why Sue had decided to leave England and when questioned I could not believe her answer. "I have fallen in love with a vet from South Africa, he has asked me to join him there when he returns to his practice in Durban."

"Have you known him long?" I asked.

A smile spread across her face, "No, only ten days." My look of disbelief must have been clear to see, as she continued, "You might have met him, he is working as a locum at the practice you use." I had a vague recollection that Neville had told me that whilst he was away he was employing an old friend from his native country. I told Sue that as I had just come back from a holiday myself, I had not paid any recent visits to the surgery. Sue said, "When we met, the earth moved for both of us, it was love at first sight."

I was unimpressed; "I think you are very brave to give up everything for a man you hardly know, but it does mean at long last I have got a Somali." Sue was undeterred by my cautious comment, and enthused about the lifestyle she would have in a foreign land. Before we left with Tibby, Sue took Liz and me outside to see her stud cats.

In one pen was a Usual Somali, whoever thought up the name Usual to describe a colour of cat should have been shot. It is far from usual, the deep gold intermingled with black is most impressive. It gives the impression of a wild cat which has swapped its natural habitat for the urban jungle. The stud was a large cat with wild green eyes. Whilst I stared in wonder at this impressive feline, something else caught my attention, his stud house. Sue had six studs, all were penned in the most up to date housing, which she had purchased only a few months earlier. I was green with envy, they were superb.

Life on the Funny Farm

After our tour of the garden, we set off for home with Tibby nestled in a soft blanket, secure in a carrier in the back of my car. I expected it would take the cat time to settle in with my Burmese, but I was wrong. Tibby strolled out of her carrier, jumped onto the sofa and began to wash herself. My other cats stared in disbelief at the confident new comer. When Graham returned home from work that evening he was greeted by Tibby who acted as though she had known him all her life. He was even more impressed when she settled down next to him as he read the daily newspaper. This was a luxury he was unaccustomed to, as the Burmese took great delight in positioning their entire body over the newsprint as one attempted to read.

Within forty-eight hours Tibby had converted my husband. He said, "I wasn't keen on you getting another cat, but I must say this breed is a lot easier to live with than the others. She isn't demanding, nor does she hurl herself around the place chasing imaginary mice."

I was pleased Tibby had won him over, because the last two days I had thought of little else but the Somalis I had left at Sue's. Now was the moment to strike! Casually I spoke, "I'm glad you like her, because I am going to see the bank manager and ask for a loan so I can buy one more female and the stud cat."

Suddenly I had Graham's complete attention, he snapped, "I don't like her that much. Don't you think you have got enough cats?" Patiently I said, "This is an opportunity too good to miss. If I had the three Somalis it would be no time at all before I could breed some kittens. I look after all the cats so it won't interfere with you."

Graham listened, a smug smile crossed his face, "You won't get your own way on this one. No bank manager is going to lend money for someone to buy a cat. Face it, Ann, it won't work."

It was my turn to smile smugly, "They will lend me the money if I say it is for cat pens, and I want to expand my business."

Graham looked horrified, "Do you really want them that badly you are prepared to incur interest charges on the loan?"

My answer was simple, "Yes I do." The thought of giving money to the bank when it was not necessary filled my husband with dismay. The solution was simple. He said, "If you are that determined I will lend you the money." I accepted his offer readily, and by the end of the week Beattie and the stud Redman had arrived.

Chapter 47 – A Somali Take-Over

Beattie settled in quickly, the same could not be said of Redman. He resided in a purpose-built stud house, and I tried to devote as much time to him as possible. This was the first stud I had owned which I had not bred myself. I had inherited him at just over three years of age; he was suspicious of my intentions, and it did not take long for me to begin to wonder if I had made a huge mistake. I could live without his affections but I could not tolerate his aggressive attitude. The last thing a new breed needed was a stud, siring kittens with dubious temperament. Redman was not adverse to flying into a rage and sinking his teeth into any available part of my body.

This behaviour continued for some weeks. It reached the point when I considered having him neutered. Just as the situation looked hopeless, there was a gradual improvement. The frequency of the attacks lessened. Redman began to shower me with affection, sitting proudly on my shoulder, busily grooming my hair with his rough tongue. He did not extend this treatment to strangers, they were still subjected to his childish tantrums, and it did not take long to realise his most aggressive attacks were aimed at women with blonde hair. I contented myself with the thought that slowly he was adjusting to life with us.

The Somalis had only been in residence a few weeks when Sue contacted me. Her plans for emigration had been finalised. She asked, "If I gave you April, the sorrel silver girl, in return could I board the seventeen cats I am taking to South Africa? It should be for no longer than a couple of weeks and by then I will have my home sorted out and their new pens erected."

This was the icing on the cake for me. I did not mind cleaning and caring for her cats if it meant I could have April, I readily agreed. Then a thought struck me, "Have you sold your stud pens yet?" I asked.

Sue replied she had not, and so we came to a deal that I purchased the pens; they were dismantled on the Friday and erected on the farm the following morning. On Sunday morning, Sue arrived with her cats and they were installed in their own houses. In the short space of time I had met Sue she had been the recipient of hundreds of pounds of my hard earned cash. I comforted myself with the knowledge I now had four Somalis and six top of the range pens. At the outset of our negotiations I made it clear that if her cats stayed longer than a

Life on the Funny Farm

fortnight she would incur boarding charges. It is not unusual for plans to be delayed a few days, but neither Sue nor I had any inkling that her cats would be with me for the next five months. When at last I waved them goodbye at Heathrow airport, I had recovered the cost of the Somalis and the pens. It was the best deal I have ever done in my life!

Chapter 48
Bovine Blunders

The arrival of the Somalis occupied my time, but in the fields the calves were growing at a dramatic speed. I needed to attend to matters; the bull calf needed to be castrated, and both calves would have to be tattooed. The Highland Cattle Society insists that all pedigree beasts are identified by a unique serial number tattooed in their ear. Neville, my vet, had ceased to treat large animals earlier in the year. Shona who preferred working with farm stock had left to join another local practice. I arranged with the new surgery that a vet would visit. I had trained the calves well I thought, for their ordeal. They were both used to the halter and would walk as well as any dog on the lead. Each day I took pains to fiddle with their ears so they would not be surprised when the vet wrote their number with his tattoo pen.

The day duly arrived for the vet's visit. My first surprise was the vet wasn't Shona, but a big burly man in his forties. He had a jolly disposition and greeted me with, "Hi cherub, what can we do for you?" I didn't realise it then, but this man was a leading expert in the field of bovine veterinary medicine. He had an air of confidence. As we strode to the field he introduced himself. "My name's Alan. It's a long time since I have dealt with Highland cattle. How are you finding the breed?"

As we walked towards the calves I chatted about my shaggy beasts. Expertly, I slipped the halters over their heads. I held Sunny, whilst Gemma controlled Oxo. Alan stood waiting. Puzzled, I asked, "Why don't you get on with the job?"

Alan stared incredulously in my direction, "I can't do the job in the middle of the field."

My first meeting with this vet was not going at all well. What was wrong with the man?" I patiently explained, "Don't worry, I have trained the calves so they are used to having a pen in their ears. It shouldn't be a problem to write the number in. We might have to hang on tight to Oxo when you castrate him, but the piglets are never a problem."

By the look on Alan's face it was clear he thought I had escaped from a lunatic asylum. In a stern no nonsense voice he said, "I don't think you have any idea how the job is done." With that, from his pocket he produced what can only be described as a large pair of pliers. On the inside were a series of letters and numbers all arranged earlier in the correct order. Alan spoke, " Tattooing animals is a painful process. They are not going to stand still while I do this, and as for the bull calf, if someone was going to part me from the company of my balls I'd put up a fight."

Over the years I have known Alan, he always says it as it is. He does not pussy foot around, but I have learnt to value his judgement. I looked around the field and asked, "Where would you like to do the job?"

Alan said, "Have you got a crush?" At least I knew what one was but did not possess such a luxury. Uncomfortably, I shook my head. Alan surveyed the farm and decided to work in the shelter. We made a makeshift pen and he set to work. My toes curled in my wellies as the tattoo device bit into the ear cartilage. The sound it made was like someone cracking their fingers but magnified twenty times over. The calves bellowed mournfully in pain. It took three of us to keep Oxo still as he was castrated, his indignant lowing echoed round the farm. My first veterinary consultation with the cattle was over but it taught me I had a lot to learn. As he left Alan could not hide his displeasure he said. "Before I come again, you had better get some basic equipment. We were lucky today we were handling calves. The bigger beasts would not have been controlled." I knew he felt he was working with an idiot. Before his next visit I would get the equipment needed and try and redeem myself.

Chapter 49
The Farm Gets a Makeover

I sought advice from my agricultural mentor, Bert. I told him, "I really want to expand the cattle, what will we need?"

Bert pushed his cap forward and deliberated a while. Thoughtfully, he said, "You must get a cattle crush so the animals can be contained when they need treatment. I suggest we put in an automatic water system and build a yard where they can be contained securely when required."

"Whatever you think is necessary had better be done, how much do you think this will all cost?" I asked. True to form Bert did not give me an estimate but worked through the summer months transforming the farm into an organised state of affairs.

It was Bert who suggested we should show the calves at a local agricultural event, the idea appealed.

The show took place at the beginning of September. We bathed Oxo and Sunny, their feet were polished, as were their tiny horns. I parted their hair along their backs, brushed their legs, backcombed their tails to make them appear square. When I had finished, they looked a picture; my years of grooming cats had stood me in good stead. The result was professional. Gemma and I loaded them in the box. Graham did the driving, and we set off to try our luck. They behaved impeccably. The public milled round them and they took it all in their stride. Both received highly commended cards. I was delighted. Next year we would attend more shows perhaps one day we would go to the Royal, but for now we would practice at the smaller meetings. Little did I know the effect our presence at the next show we attended would have!

The calves were growing into adolescent beasts. It was time to mate Tess and Sonasag. As we didn't have a bull I decided to use artificial insemination. I looked through a catalogue of bulls whose semen was stored by the firm, and selected a likely sire for my next calves. Our newly acquired crush was soon put to use and both girls were served. I did not have to wait long to discover if they were pregnant, the operation had only resulted in Tess conceiving. Sonasag must have enjoyed her date with the AI man as the procedure had to be repeated.

October was fast approaching. We had received details of the autumn sale of Highland cattle, which is held annually in Oban. Graham and I decided to go. It coincided with the half term holiday so we decided to take the children with us. The show and sale would last for two days. We booked accommodation in Oban but we planned to visit Edinburgh first for a few days. Our stay in the Scottish capital was enjoyable; we took the children to the castle and we visited the tourist attractions. We left after a few days and wended our way to the small town of Oban. Immediately, I fell in love with the West coast. It was my first visit to this part of Scotland but its beauty was breathtaking. We visited the harbour to watch the ferries laden with Highland cattle approach the mainland. These cattle had come from the severe terrain of the Western Islands. Twice a year this scene was re-enacted. The cattle were then taken to the Mart where their stockmen and women bedded them down for the night. The next morning, they would have to busy themselves preparing them for the show. Until then it was time for the humans to let their hair down.

Many of the people only left the islands for the cattle sales, and Oban was the equivalent of a large city, with its pubs and parties. Many of the stockmen stayed at the same hotel as us and we chatted companionably through the evening, learning the tricks of the trade. Most of them did not have strong Scottish accents as in the islands Gaelic is the national language and English, the second, so they spoke very precisely. All too soon, the evening was over and we retired to our bed. I couldn't wait for the show the next day. In the catalogue I had read about a white Highlander carrying a calf to the top bull of the day. I had designs on purchasing her. Graham was lying next to me, blissfully unaware of my plans!

Chapter 50
Highland Fling

The next morning we left the hotel and made our way to the Mart. It was a hive of activity as the stockmen busied themselves preparing their cattle for a moment of glory in the show ring. All the beasts were immaculately turned out, their horns and feet shone. The air was filled with the scent of shampoo as their coats glistened, the fur rippled as they walked around the arena. Every colour of the breed was represented, red, yellow, black, and white. My attention was drawn to the cow I hoped to buy. All I had to do now was sell the idea to Graham!

I began, "That is nice looking cow. I wouldn't mind owning a white one."

Graham studied the cow, "It doesn't look very special to me. I must say it is fun just to come and look, and not buy anything for a change."

I realised some persuasion would be needed, "There would be no harm in bidding for her tomorrow in the sale. She is fourteen years old and that will put a lot of people off. What really interests me is she is carrying a calf to the top bull. Imagine the quality heifer we could have."

Graham looked resigned as he said, "It seems to me you have researched this cow long before we came here. You have forgotten one little detail, how would we get her home?" Confidently I replied, "I'm sure we could sort that out, during the day I'll ask around. If I can find someone to transport her, shall we bid for her?"

Graham sighed, "I suppose so, but we are not spending a lot of money. If she fetches a high price you can forget it."

I agreed readily, I then spent the morning finding someone to transport her. The journey home from Oban would be too long for a beast. I found a farmer in Cheshire who agreed if I bought a cow he would transport it to his farm. The animal would rest there overnight, and we would collect her the next day. The problem was solved. All I had to do now was secure her at the right price.

The show finished in the afternoon. A dinner dance had been arranged for the evening, so we retired to the hotel to don our glad rags for the Society bash. All the members gathered for the meal, the main course was none other than beef, which was ceremoniously piped in to the tune Scotland the Brave. Once the meal was over people made their way to the bar and dance floor. Within minutes, the Scottish band began to play and the room was filled with whirling kilts and whoops of delight as the islanders partied with gusto. Graham and I managed to conquer the Gay Gordons but the rest was out of our league. Lucy watched the dancers with fascination, she became restless and asked, "Can I dance, Mummy?" She was a good little dancer and attended tap dancing lessons. The reels were well beyond my ability so I asked one of the Scottish members if she would dance with her. The lady said her dancing days were over but she would try and find someone who would guide her through the moves.

Shortly after, an elderly gentleman appeared and asked Lucy to join him for the eightsome reel. The diminutive figure of Lucy stepped out onto the dance floor, The Scottish tartans representing the different clans surrounded the purple and black velvet dress she wore. She began tentatively, watching the dancers' moves. It did not take her long to master the reel and within a short while was giving the other dancers a run for their money! So much so she danced the evening away, receiving genuine admiration from the natives. In the early hours of the morning we returned to the hotel and quickly fell to sleep.

We awoke the next morning and headed for the sale. The white cow came into the ring, and as I had predicted, there was little interest in her. I was now quite used to auctions. It was a very sedate affair, and before I knew it I was the proud owner of Milly. The transport arrangements were put into action and the following evening she was settled at our farm. She had only been with us a short while be-

Chapter 50- Highland Fling

fore she calved. I was quite right she gave birth to a top class calf, but sadly it was a bull calf, not the heifer I desired. I named the little white bull calf, Jock.

Chapter 51
A Surprise Christmas Present

We were well into winter, the days were shortened, I began work in the morning surrounded by the dark. Occasionally, the stars twinkled in the sky. The colder months made life on the farm more taxing, I was always glad when I could retreat indoors and settle by the fire playing with a litter of kittens. My Burmese, Fleur had five kittens and all were brown in colour. Unlike moggies pedigree cats tend to breed all the year round. The moggy has an inbuilt awareness that rearing a litter in the winter months is nothing short of folly. Their pedigree counterparts lead a cosseted existence and have no such reservations. I have always been opposed to selling kittens as Christmas presents, not just because they may be discarded as an unwanted gift, but usually during the festive season the normal household routine is disrupted, hardly the best time to introduce a new family member who craves stability. Fleur's litter would be ready to leave at Christmas but I had decided the new owners would have to wait until the New Year.

At the end of November I took the kittens to the vet for the start of their vaccination programme. Angus was on duty, carefully he examined each kitten and inoculated them. He always took time with the babes, playing with each individual, one kitten in particular grabbed his attention.

"What's this kitten called?" he asked.

Slightly embarrassed I answered, "Willy Wonka."

Angus smiled broadly, "Sounds as though Joe and Lucy have had a hand in naming this litter."

Chapter 51 - A Surprise Christmas Present

I agreed and told him that all the litter had names of characters in children's books. I often let the kids name them as it gave them a sense of involvement, usually they chose acceptable names but I did draw the line when Joe wanted to call one Battle Cat after a cartoon character. I felt it did not quite conjure up the right image.

As Angus continued to play with the kitten he spoke, "Shona has always wanted a Burmese, she grew up with them as a child. This wee chap has plenty of personality, would you consider selling him to us?" I was delighted, I could think of no better parents for one of my babies than two qualified vets. I readily agreed.

Angus said, "I want this to be a surprise, can I collect him Christmas Eve when I finish at the surgery?"

Without hesitation I replied, "I don't let my kittens go at Christmas but in your case I will make an exception. If Shona calls I won't say a word I promise you."

The days passed by quickly, and Christmas would soon be here. Peanuts was due to have his routine tetanus and flu jab, the vet who arrived to vaccinate him was none other than Shona. Peanuts was now a picture of health and was being schooled in the basics of good horse manners. Shona was impressed with his progress. Sshe vaccinated him, and I invited her in for a cup of tea. The day was cold and wet so she was pleased to have some respite from the elements. She walked into the sitting room and was greeted by Fleur and the babies. I left her playing with them as I made the drinks. On my return she was still engrossed with the feline family. As I entered, she looked up and said, "Are any of these kittens looking for a home?"

I shook my head, "No they are all spoken for, they will be leaving me just after Christmas."

She said thoughtfully, "They must have had the first part of their inoculations, who vaccinated them?"

I was beginning to feel uncomfortable as I replied, "Angus did the consultation."

Shona could not hide her annoyance, "He knows I want a kitten, he could have booked one when he saw them. I shall tell him what I think of him when I get home."

Any doubts I may have had that Shona wanted a kitten were dispelled immediately, but I did feel very sorry for Angus having to face his irate wife. Angus phoned the next morning to tell me Shona was barely speaking to him, but it would all be worth it on Christmas Eve. He chuckled at the thought of her remorse and wondered how she would seek his forgiveness.

Perhaps it is a sign of increasing age when Christmas seems to come quicker every year and this time was no exception. True to his word Angus collected Willie when the surgery closed. Within the hour the phone rang, I heard the exuberant voice of Shona, "How ever did you not give the game away the other week? It is the best present ever, we shall love him to bits I promise." I had no doubt about it. It is very rewarding to be able to settle a kitten into a new family and this time it had given me even greater pleasure. I hoped they would enjoy Willie's company for the next fifteen years at least.

Chapter 52
Biting Off More than You Can Chew

Joe and Lucy were excited at the prospect of Christmas Day and opening their presents, eventually they were packed off to bed, and before long Graham and I retired too. Just before midnight Lucy woke me with her crying. I went into her bedroom to discover what was wrong. Through the sobs she told me her ear hurt.

Poor old Lucy, earache just as Christmas morn dawned. I went into the kitchen to get her some pain relief and to warm a bottle. While I was preparing everything the phone rang. I looked at the kitchen wall clock, it was twelve-thirty. My stomach churned, the phone ringing at this time of the night usually meant trouble, I hoped all the family were safe and well. With dread I picked up the receiver and heard a voice I did not recognise.

"Hello, is that Ann?"

"Yes. Who am I speaking to?"

"Oh, thank goodness. It's Mrs. Brown I board my miniature Dachshund, Billy with you."

I couldn't believe a customer was on the phone at this time in the morning, whatever could she want?

"I have tried to ring a vet but there is no answer, Billy has chewed the electric cable of the Christmas tree lights. He let out a dreadful scream and ran into his basket, I don't know what to do."

Life on the Funny Farm

Curtly, I said, "You would let out a yell if two hundred and forty vaults went through your mouth. Keep an eye on him, make sure he doesn't go into shock, and keep him warm and quiet. Make sure his breathing is steady. If he starts to have any difficulties you will have to keep trying to get the vet. As he was able to run into his basket I think you will find he will soon be his old self."

The relief in Mrs. Brown's voice was audible, "Thank you, I just didn't know who to ring. There is just one more thing, when Billy bit through the wire, it fused all the electrics in my house. You don't know how I can sort that out do you?"

Amazed I was involved in such a conversation, I simply said, "You need an electrician for that, but I doubt you will get any response at this time. It is Christmas Day you know." As I replaced the receiver I smiled to myself, a cattery and kennel owner is never off duty. You never know what the next phone call will bring.

Our small fold of highland cattle now numbered seven beasts. It was becoming increasingly difficult to round them up to move them into new fields. It was a natural progression to look for a dog that would be able to work the cattle. Zac was a wonderful protector but had no herding instincts. Sally was definitely a pipe and slippers dog. What we needed was a Collie. I approached my friend, Tony at the local rescue centre and asked him to keep a look out for a suitable dog. It was not long before Tony phoned to say he had the ideal candidate. I visited the sanctuary to see for myself.

Tony introduced me to Bess, a pedigree Border Collie who had worked on a farm. Sadly her master had died and she was now redundant. There was no doubt she was well trained and obedient but in the presence of the other dogs she tried to assert her dominance, I knew Zac would not tolerate such behaviour. I gave Tony my decision, "I'm sorry, but she won't fit in with my other dogs. She is a beautiful creature, intelligent. She would have been ideal in every other respect." Tony accepted my decision, and we walked out of the kennel block into the yard. We coincidentally timed our exit with a bunch of dogs returning from a romp in the paddock. Before I knew what was happening a muddy, excitable collie type dog bounded up to me, totally undisciplined and it then proceeded to leap around me. Tony called the dog away, but it was having none of it. I studied the dog more closely; it was a black and white bitch, clearly totally

Chapter 52 – Biting Off More Than You Can Chew

mad and untrained. Then I noticed the liquid brown eyes. They stared at me with trust, and gentleness. I turned to Tony and said, "Is this dog available?"

Tony was dismayed, "She is but you don't want that one, she's as mad as a hatter."

I was not going to be deterred, "What is her history?"

With resignation in his voice he said, "She is eight months old, her name is Scampi. She lived in a town house and the owners brought her here because she attacked their five-year-old son. In fairness, I must say we have never seen any aggression, but you can never tell."

I looked once more into her eyes; I could not believe she had an aggressive streak. We agreed that I should take her home on a month's trial. Tony shouted as we left, "You'll be back within the week!"

Once home I realised the dog knew nothing, not even her name. She could run as fast as a greyhound, she hurtled around the farm at great speed, flying here and there.

I did not like the name she had been given so I renamed her Fly. She was a quick learner; within a fortnight she would sit, lie down, and stay, she was eager to please her new mistress. She showed no signs of aggression, but she did crave attention. If I was busy working and she wanted to attract my attention she would creep up behind and give my bottom a nip, as if to say, "I'm still here." She did have one major vice, and I am sure this was the real reason the original owners parted company with her. She was very destructive, in the first three months she managed to eat her way through a kitchen cupboard, the plaster from the walls and the linoleum floor covering. It took twelve months to break her of the habit.

Fly was trustworthy around the other animals. I began her training with the ducks. At first when given the away command she would run hell for leather into their midst, scattering them to the four corners of the farm. Slowly but surely, she learnt to herd them, manipulating them in the desired direction. She loved to work, and even to this day she is never happier than when we are working side by side on the farm. Months after her arrival Tony called in for a chat. He could not believe the transformation in the dog, over the years it still continued to amaze him.

Chapter 53
Duped at an Auction

February arrived, and once more we set off to a cattle auction in the Midlands. I did not know it then, but I was about to buy my last cow at auction, and in the process learn a lesson I would never forget. Many of the beasts present were not of the same calibre as those we had seen at the Scottish sale. The buyers realised this and the bidding was reluctant. Graham and I sat at the ringside. I made the fatal mistake of getting engrossed in conversation with my neighbour. Graham urgently tugged at my coat and said, "Bid for this cow, no one seems interested in her. She is only six years old, in calf, she is the bargain of the day." I should have known better, my partner has many attributes but he has no natural eye for animals. I did as instructed and with out any competition the cow named, Barnaigh of Evelyn was sold to me. Graham was delighted she had only cost five hundred guineas, in Highland Cattle terms a snip!

My first feeling of foreboding began when I went to meet the owner and inspect my purchase. The owner looked me up and down and warned, "She doesn't like anyone fussing around her head, and be careful of the back legs she has been known to kick." That managed to cover all the angles, her horn span was one of the largest I had ever seen on a Highlander, and looking down at her feet I could imagine the bruising experience they could inflict. After all the warnings I was amazed how well she went into the box for the journey home. An hour later we arrived at the farm. We drove the transporter into the yard, intending to unload her and keep her in the yard over night. When I opened the side door the sight that greeted me filled me with

Chapter 53 - Duped at an Auction

horror. Her eyes were rolling in her head; she was foaming at the mouth like a rabid beast. In her struggle to become free the halter had become so tight I could not loosen it. Each time I ventured into the box she lunged at me, murder in her eyes. I shouted to Graham to assist me, he peered into the box and exclaimed, "What the hell's the matter with her?"

Irritably I replied, "How do I know? Perhaps she didn't like your driving."

We made repeated attempts to free the halter, but all to no avail. At last Graham said, "There is nothing for it but to cut through the rope, then we'll lower the ramp down and drive her into the yard." It seemed a good idea at the time, so we cut the halter, lowered the ramp, but the rest of the plan never had a chance to be put into action!

The incensed cow rampaged out of the box, horns and feet flailing in every direction, she charged in a straight line towards the field gate. Before either of us could do anything, she raised herself on her powerful hind legs and jumped clean over the five bar gate. Once in the field she hurtled around, bellowing for all she was worth.

Graham shell shocked from the experience turned to me and quietly asked, "What the hell have we bought?"

Grimly, I replied, "A lot of trouble by the looks of it. I shall see how she is in the morning, but I think we can safely say she had been doped for that sale. No wonder no one bid for her; with their experience they must have known. We pair of dopes walked straight in. You were right about one thing she is a bargain, one we didn't expect!"

The next morning I went to the field, dreading what I might find, but the new addition was grazing peacefully with the others. Perhaps she would settle after all. Now, the effects of the drugs had worn off. I decided to take a closer look, no sooner had I walked a few feet into the field than she raised her head watching my moves closely. I was studying her closely too, the tell tale signs began to appear. Her head went down, a loud bellow echoed across the paddock, I was already in retreat before she began her charge! The time had come to call the cavalry: Within the hour, Bert arrived. One glance at the cow was enough. Bert said, "You got a wrongun there, Anna. She is wild, she might mellow in time but you will have to be very careful."

As always, Bert was right. Eventually she calmed down but I never took any liberties with her. She always had a mean streak and I named her accordingly, Evie the evil one! I later discovered it was not an unusual practice to sedate an awkward cow for the sale ring, it was a risk I was not prepared to take again, once bitten twice shy.

Chapter 54
Graham is Put Through His Paces

Spring had arrived. I was determined to show the cattle more often so we entered a show at Ashby de la Zouch, which was near to the town where I grew up. We took Oxo and Sunny. Gemma came along as did my children. As usual, Graham was chauffeur. Tom and Emily agreed to meet us there and brought along some childhood friends of mine. I wanted to show the beasts off in all their glory to my friends. We took a picnic lunch, and we had planned our strategy. Gemma would take Oxo around the ring, and I would take Sunny. As usual the beasts looked well groomed, every part of their bodies gleamed. So we did not let them down, we had invested in two sparkling white overalls. We were ready and full of expectation.

As soon as we got there we ran into problems. Most people had already arrived. To get to our stalls we had to park a distance away, and then walk the cattle through rows of lorries and assorted vehicles. It was not an easy task. Sonny was nervous, and as I tried to persuade her to go in one direction she pulled in the other. As a consequence I severely bruised my right arm against a lorry. Within a short space of time it became very painful. I knew I would not be able to control Sonny in the ring.

Gemma had Oxo to worry about. It was no use I would have to ask Graham to come to our rescue. Much to my surprise, Graham did not seem concerned at the request. He said, "I've watched you training them in the yard. There doesn't look anything to it. The only problem is – what shall I wear?"

Life on the Funny Farm

I was a little worried by his confidence. There is a saying never work with kids or animals and there is a good reason, you never know what they will do next! However, the problem of attire was soon sorted. "You can wear my overall, it won't be perfect but it will suffice."

Graham spluttered, "I shall look a bloody fool. You aren't even five foot. I'm nearer six feet tall."

"It can't be helped." With that, I took the coat off and he tried it on. The length was short and the full-length sleeves gave the impression of a short-sleeved garment. The buttons would not meet, but despite all that, it could have been worse.

As we stood waiting for our class to be called I gave my new stockman some pointers.

"Keep her close to the other beasts. She will happily follow them around. Keep a tight hold of the halter, and use your stick to make her stand square."

Graham snapped, "For goodness' sake, Ann, I've seen you practice enough. If you can do it then it will be a doddle for me."

I did not share his confidence, I knew my beasts and what they were capable of, and Graham had a strong belief in himself; in his own mind there was nothing he couldn't do. Sadly these ideas were often misguided. My partner was about to stare humiliation in the face! The public address system crackled into life. Our class was being called to the ring. With huge misgivings, I watched my heifer walk steadily in to the arena with my husband in tow.

I stood at the ringside flanked by Tom and Emily. Joe, Lucy and our friends milled round. The class was large. The judge asked for the beasts to walk around the ring. The judge paid particular attention to their movement and the overall impression of the beasts. All was going well. Graham was following my instructions to the letter, keeping Sunny close to the cow in front. Apart from the ill-fitting overall they looked good. After the judge had seen them all move he asked the exhibitors to line their cattle up. Once again, like a trooper my husband settled Sunny into the line. He even managed to get her to stand correctly. Slowly, the judge worked his way down the line. Sunny was positioned halfway down. At last, he reached her and examined her thoroughly. He then moved on to the next competitor. Laboriously, he inspected the remaining beasts.

Chapter 54 – Graham is Put Through His Paces

My eyes were fixed on Sunny and Graham. To my horror, I saw disaster looming. My husband stood relaxed. He had taken his eye off the ball. Sunny glanced in his direction and instinctively knew he was not concentrating. He was in a world of his own! Sunny took her chance and broke ranks. The sudden tug on the halter alerted my stockman to impending disaster. It was too late; he could not stop the half-ton of beast, which was now careering out of control. The judge engrossed in his task knew nothing of what was happening behind him. Sunny decided to attract his attention in the only way she knew how. She had increased her speed to a canter. Graham was hanging on helplessly to the rope three feet behind her. With well timed accuracy she reached the judge and with one deft flick of her head she raised him from the ground, his posterior wedged between her horns. She lowered her head and the judge tumbled to the ground. The crowd laughed loudly, some even thought the escapade had been staged to provide comic relief. Worse was to come, the other cows in the class decided to join in the fray. They began to break free from the handlers, the result was pandemonium. The judge picked himself up, and through the mayhem spied the guilty parties. In a loud voice he shouted, "You are disqualified." Graham did not need to be told twice, with his dented ego, and ill-fitting overall he marched Sunny out of the ring with as much dignity as he could muster. He came straight towards me, leaving the onlookers no doubt as to who owned the wayward beast. Through clenched teeth he said, "I will never take a beast in a ring again, don't ever ask me." To this day, he has never repeated the experience. From that day on he has watched with grudging admiration as I train the beasts for the show ring.

Once again we didn't win any prizes, but we did supply entertainment for the crowd. The next year we were invited to attend the show again, but I declined the offer. If we were going to make fools of ourselves, better it was in front of strangers than friends!

Chapter 55
A Load of Bull

Summer was now in full swing, the kennels and cattery were full to bursting point. Every moment of the day was devoted to the care of the animals and my human family. The calves were growing at a rate of knots. It was time to castrate the bull calves. Jock was developing into a fine specimen of the breed, and on each visit to the farm Bert was impressed by the young bull calf. So much so, he said, "Anna, it would be a crying shame to castrate the calf." I knew instinctively where the conversation was leading. The only experience I had of bulls was in my teenage years. I spent most of my free time in those days with friends who lived on a large arable and cattle farm. They had two bulls, one a Fresian called Fred, and a Hereford. Timmy was a gentle soul, typical of his breed that loved nothing more than having his chin scratched. On the other hand Fred was an evil sod, whose only desire in life was to kill or maim any human being, who got in his way. The thought of owning my own bull did not fill me with confidence. Bert had given the matter a great deal of thought and was going to give me his opinion whether I wanted it or not.

He began, "Anna, you have had problems getting the cows pregnant using AI. You have already arranged to loan a bull, at least if you keep this young chap you will know all about his foibles." It was true that I was soon to welcome a bull onto the farm. He was only going to stay a few weeks. Once he had served the cows I would return him to his owner. It was a very different matter to have a bull

Chapter 55 - A Load of Bull

around all the time. I decided I would ask Graham what he thought about it!

I told my husband about Bert's suggestion, his reaction was predictable. "What in hell's name will he think of next? We only have four cows. I can't see them keeping a virile bull happy for long. Think of the cost of keeping him. No, Ann. Stick with the AI or hire someone else's then they can have the worry and expense." For a change, I agreed with him, but I decided to keep my options open and delay the unkindest cut of all to the male of the species. The immediate problem was resolved the following week when a huge brindle coloured bull arrived on loan. Alec was a formidable creature, without a backward glance he walked out of the lorry and into the field where the cows were waiting. He got down to business straight away, and within six weeks he had served all the females. His sheer size was intimidating, and while he was with us I treated him with great respect. I was relieved when the time came for him to return home. I had not learnt to trust him, and my caution was well founded. The night before his departure we decided to move him into the yard. Bert agreed to help. Alec was reluctant to leave his women, but Bert tempted him away from them with a bucket feed. As so often happens, the weather was atrocious; rain pelted down on us as we walked through the fields. I had donned my waterproofs, and my trusty large brimmed hat, which served as an umbrella. At a steady pace the bull approached the yard, but at the last moment he decided he would prefer to return to the field. When confronted by a ton of muscular animal that has his mind set on his own agenda, life can become difficult.

With the help of Gemma, Bert and I tried to turn him round. For a large animal he spun round with agility and stared in my direction.

Until then he had been no trouble at all, but now his whole demeanour changed. He began to paw the ground, snorting aggressively, and there was no question what had grabbed his attention. As he headed straight towards me, Bert shouted, "Anna, it's your hat, he doesn't like it." I didn't need telling twice, I wrenched it from my head, and flung it as far away as I could. It took on the properties of a Frisbee as it sailed through the air. The bull stood amazed as the hat flew past his head. Bert took advantage of his surprise and deftly drove

Life on the Funny Farm

him into the secure yard. With legs like jelly and shaking hands I retrieved my hat from the mud covered ground. The next morning Alec was collected, and I was relieved to see him go. After that experience I knew I would not hire a bull again. From now on, it was either the AI man or my cows would be left to the tender mercies of my little white bull, Jock.

Chapter 56
Waifs and Strays

That summer saw the arrival of a number of new additions, most were uninvited. Early one morning as I busied myself feeding the stock, I heard the familiar mewing of a kitten. It did not take me long to discover the forlorn babe among the hay bales. It was a male tabby kitten with white bib and socks. I estimated his age to be nine weeks. We took care of him, and tried to find out where he had come from. No one claimed ownership, which was hardly a surprise as over the years we have found many abandoned animals on the farm. One evening someone tied a dog to our gate with a note saying, 'We don't want this anymore, find a home for it.' That, we were able to do. On another occasion I awoke to discover a goat tethered in the field, also with a note round its neck proclaiming 'My name is Baby'. Baby joined the rest of my herd of goats and spent many happy years with us. As no one wanted the tabby kitten, Joe who had become very attached to him asked if we could keep him. I agreed, and my son named him Sami.

Sami took no time at all to settle into life on the farm. He had a cheeky sense of humour, a devil take care attitude to life. He became a fearless hunter and to this day I have never owned a cat with his hunting skills. He was so quick he managed to control the number of moles which were hell bent on ruining my large lawn with their maze of tunnels. Nothing frightened Sami; he had a belief in his own invincibility. The only animal on the farm he did not like was my Burmese stud Bill. Sami would spend a large part of his day sitting

Life on the Funny Farm

outside Bill's house, taunting him with his freedom. To rub salt into the wounds further, Sami would line up his trophies outside the pen. It was not unusual for me to find an assortment of mice, moles and shrews neatly placed in full view of Bill.

Sami soon became a firm favourite of the customers; as soon as the reception bell rang he would appear and investigate the new arrival. It did not matter to him whether it was feline or canine. All would be subjected to his scrutiny. As far as Sami was concerned customers cars were also in need of his appraisal. He would leap in the opened door and immediately settle down on the seats, trying them out for comfort. For most of my customers this caused amusement, but one lady took exception. It was her first visit. She arrived with her cat in a brand new Rolls Royce.

The woman clearly thought as much of her car as she did of herself. Sami treated her to his usual greeting and leapt on to the plush leather back seat. It was clear that Sami thought this was some kind of car, the soft hide was just too much of a temptation as he extended his claws and dug them into the yielding material. To say the woman had a fit would be putting it mildly; she only boarded her cat with us once, but Sami never lost us anymore customers. In fact, regular customers were dismayed when he was busy on Safari and failed to greet them.

Hunting can be a dangerous occupation, and it was not long before Sami met his Waterloo, in the shape of a squirrel. One lunch time the phone rang. I picked up the receiver to hear a man's voice on the other end, "I'm ringing from the car compound next door. Have you got a tabby and white cat?" Next to the farm was a huge depot where cars were stored awaiting sale from the Rover group. The security was tight and a high fence topped with rows of barbed wire surrounded the whole complex to deter intruders. I told the caller I had a tabby cat with white socks and a bib. He then went on to inform me, "That sounds like your cat. We saw him chasing a squirrel. His quarry cleared the fence, but I'm afraid your cat didn't manage to do the same. At present he is impaled on the barbed wire." I replaced the phone and called to Gemma. We set off to the rescue. I dreaded what we might find. Sure enough he was well and truly ensnared. With the help of the men at the depot, carefully we freed him. I took him directly to Neville, who examined him carefully. He said, "Amaz-

Chapter 56 – Waifs and Strays

ingly he does not seem to have done any major damage to his body. His thick fur has meant the wounds are only skin deep. However, he has broken his tail in three places. Unfortunately I will have to amputate it. He will only have a stub remaining."

The next day Sami underwent surgery and when I brought him home he resembled a Manx cat. Within days he was back on form, hunting as well as ever. I thought his experience might have taught him to stay well clear of squirrels, but it was not to be. Sami for the rest of his life had a score to settle with the squirrel population; every time he managed to catch one, he would systematically remove their tail and keep the trophy as a plaything. I think one could say he was getting his own back!

In the summer months, there is a constant stream of customers arriving and the phone rings at all times of the day and night. It was no surprise that one morning at six o'clock I was interrupted from my work by the shrill ringing. I answered the call; on the line was a distressed man. It was Mr. Smith, an elderly gentleman who was one of our regular customers. It took me some moments before I could understand what he was trying to tell me. In between his heart wrenching sobs, I heard him say, "I woke up this morning to find my wife dead beside me. I don't know what to do, I have called the doctor but I can't cope with the cats. Can you board them for me until everything is sorted?"

I quickly reassured him that we would look after his cats for as long as necessary. I also realised he had a need to talk to someone. He was alone with his wife's body waiting for help to arrive. For the next thirty minutes I sat and listened, offering what little comfort I could in a phone conversation. At last, I heard his door bell ring and knew the doctor had arrived. He had no means of transport so I arranged for a member of staff to collect the cats as soon as possible. I rang Liz and asked her to fetch his pets on her way to the farm. I explained the situation to her. In a short while Liz drove in to the farm with the cats. She quickly got out of the car and strode purposefully towards me. In a loud voice she said, "Don't ever ask me to do anything like that again. I timed my arrival with the mortuary van, it was awful. Mr. Smith was so distressed. I didn't know what to say." I too hoped that the experience would never be repeated. Two weeks later Mr. Smith collected his cats, and over the years they were able to of-

Life on the Funny Farm

fer him some companionship and solace in the lonely evenings after his wife's demise.

Chapter 57
Raffles

Throughout the summer the population of farm animals continued to increase. My goats and pig gave birth uneventfully to more young. The rooster Cocky managed with the help of the hens to add to our flock. My cats were busy too, and Tibby gave birth to our first litter of Somalis. Kittens have always enchanted me but these were unbelievably pretty. They looked as though they had stepped off the lid of a chocolate box. She gave birth to three kittens, a blue, and two fawns, all were boys. Months earlier I had told Lucy she could have a kitten of her very own, the choice would be hers. As the kittens grew I noticed the blue kitten was not thriving as well as the others. Matters came to a head one morning when I noticed his eyes had a yellow tinge. I took him to Neville, who diagnosed he had a failing liver. The prognosis was not good; there was little chance of survival. I am a great believer in where there is life there is hope, so he received treatment and I took him home for intensive nursing. As soon as I entered the house Lucy greeted me, she asked, "What did the vet say?"

I replied, "He is a very sick kitten, it is unlikely he will survive but we will do our best."

Lucy scooped the frail kitten into her arms and said, "Mummy, you said I could have a kitten of my very own, I want this one. I'll look after him and make him better."

My stomach churned, young children have an inherent belief in happy endings. All I could foresee was misery for my daughter. I tried to dissuade her, "Lucy, why don't you have one of his brothers? Even if he lives it is more than likely he will be a sickly cat for the rest of his life."

Lucy was adamant, "I want this one, and he will be alright just you wait and see."

The determination on her face convinced me there was no point in arguing with her. She made a bed for him in her bedroom and that was the beginning of an extraordinary relationship between feline and child. Lucy kept her word and nursed the kitten, which we called Raffles, night and day. Wherever Lucy went Raffles was there also. They ate, slept, and watched television together. Each day, we took him to the vet for medication, and each day Neville shook his head and said the jaundice was not improving, the outlook was bleak.

A week later I was woken by Lucy screaming for me to come to her bedroom. As I ran to her room I feared the worst; had Raffles given up his fight for life?

My mind was racing, how would I console my daughter? Living on a farm the children, from a very early age, had realised that death is always lurking in the midst of life. When Lucy was only four years old she had found a duckling dead in the pond. She had brought the sodden body to me. With her arms outstretched she had held the lifeless bird towards me and said, "Mummy, mend the duck." That was when she discovered mothers were only human. I felt inadequate then, and I felt acutely the despair she would be feeling now. With great trepidation I walked into her room. Lucy stood there, a huge grin spreading across her face. She announced, "Look at Raffles he isn't yellow anymore." I studied the kitten myself, and sure enough his mouth and ears were a beautiful healthy pink. I did not wish to dampen Lucy's exhilaration, but we had won the battle not the war.

Over the next few weeks Raffles continued to improve. Neville informed us that the liver is capable of regenerating so there was every reason to believe that he would survive. However, the vet warned us his young body had been tested to the limits and it was unlikely he would see old age. Lucy was unconcerned; she had got him this far and in the eyes of a child the future was a long way off.

Tibby was not my only Somali to be nursing a litter of kittens. April the Sorrel silver girl was nursing two babies. April was an extremely affectionate cat, and at every given opportunity would wind

Chapter 57 - Raffles

herself around people's legs. There was many a time when I would nearly break my own leg trying to avoid treading on her. One morning Gemma and I were busy feeding her and the kittens, when April wound herself around Gemma's legs. My kennel maid lost her balance, and as she fell she trod on April. The cat let out unearthly screams as she hurtled around the room. Within seconds the walls were covered with blood. With great difficulty I managed to pick her up. I knew immediately the injury was very serious, I shouted to Gemma, "Ring the vet and tell them I am on my way with an emergency."

I bundled the cat into the car and drove at break neck speed towards expert help. I could hear her rasping breathing in the car and feared she would be dead on arrival. I was convinced she had broken her neck. At the vets Angus was waiting for me, the consulting room had been cleared ready for our arrival. April was deeply shocked and Angus found it difficult to examine her but at last he told me the situation. "She has broken her jaw in two places. I can repair one of the breaks but the other is inoperable. If I wire that one she will have no mobility of the jaw. The right eye has sustained damage. If we are lucky we might be able to save it."

I was stunned; I could not believe that a human foot in a plimsoll could inflict such damage. Hesitantly I asked, "Can you save her?" Angus looked at the terrified cat and said, "I'll do my very best." And that was exactly what he did. With great skill the jaw and eye were reconstructed. For weeks she could only eat pureed food, but the resilience of animals never ceases to amaze me and in a short space of time she was eating normally again. The eye was repaired so well the damage was not visible. Angus had saved her life, and he earned my undying gratitude. It came as a personal blow when he informed me he was going to leave the practice and return to the North of Britain. I often think back to the day I first met him, when he announced he had little time for cat breeders. Over the years he and Shona had become my friends. I would miss them both dreadfully. To this day we have kept in touch, and every Christmas I receive a card detailing the antics of their by now, very elderly Burmese cat.

Chapter 58
Ducking and Diving

Meg continued to be a frequent visitor. We attended many shows together through the summer months. One day she brought with her another of her father's surplus to requirements; a feathered friend. It was a black Indian Runner duck. We had various types of ducks already – charming miniature Call Ducks, the large, cumbersome Muscovy ducks, the equally large white Aylsbury ducks, but this new addition was certainly different. He had a long neck and an upright stance. It did not take me long to find out why they were called Indian Runners. He could move like the wind when he wanted to. The staff all thought he looked like a beer bottle and so we named him BB. He had a voracious sexual appetite and after his arrival most of the ducks hatched on the farm were part runners. He was extremely generous with his genes. My other drakes found his intervention with their women disconcerting but how ever hard they tried to thwart his advances they failed, as he was far too quick for them. The females found his speed frightening and the saying 'sitting duck' took on a whole new meaning.

It was not long after BB's arrival that another bird paid us a visit. Usually, the cattle grazed lazily in the field, but one afternoon they became agitated and began to run round the fields. Gemma and I went to investigate. Soon we realised they were attacking something black. As we approached we could see it was a huge bird. We could not leave things as they were, so with a great deal of effort we managed to capture the bird. To our surprise it was a cormorant, it

Chapter 58 – Ducking and Diving

offered little resistance as it was worn out. Earlier that week we had endured high winds. We assumed he had been blown off course and had lost his way. We made a makeshift pen and settled the bird into his temporary home. I consulted my bird books and his plumage matched that of an adolescent bird. I went to the local supermarket and bought him some whole mackerel. The bird had a formidable beak, so I fed him the fish with a pair of barbecue tongs. We named him Colin. He stayed with us for a couple of weeks until we could find him a home at a sanctuary, which had other cormorants. During that time he cost me a fortune in fish, but his arrival certainly caused a stir.

Summer was now drawing to a close. Raffles had fared well through the summer months, but now as the cooler weather approached I noticed his fur was becoming sparse. I decided to visit Neville as most of my cats were now growing their thicker coats ready for the winter months. Neville was not greatly concerned. He said it was a side effect of all the medication he had received earlier in the year. Eventually his fur would grow. It didn't. Instead, it continued to drop out until the only fur remaining was on his head. I worried that he would catch a chill so we cut a sleeve off a pink jumper and made a woolly jacket for him. Raffles with his overcoat was a topic of conversation with our visitors. It was then Lucy dropped her next bombshell. She announced, "Mummy, I've been thinking, I would like to take Raffles to a show." I looked at the comical figure of the cat in front of me and laughed, "I don't think you will ever be able to show him, just be glad you still have him."

Lucy was not to be deterred, "I know he can't go to a show at the moment, but you wait when his fur grows back he will go."

Lucy must have been to Raffles what the fairy Godmother was to Cinderella, because some months later not only did he attend a show but he also won his open class. Over the years Lucy showed her beloved Raffles. Whether he won or lost did not matter to her, she always took the best cat home with her at the end of the show.

Chapter 59
Sex in the Country

The cows were now heavily pregnant and soon calving would begin again. Our Heifer Sunny, although too young to be mated, had become sexually aware. Her desire to seek a mate drove her to escape from the confines of the field and set off in search of a handsome bull. I was blissfully unaware she was AWOL until early one morning I received a call from the car depot next door. Sonny had paid them a visit. A group of drivers had surrounded her, prepared to keep her contained until I could arrive. Graham and I set off in hot pursuit, I took her halter with me, as it was more than likely we would have to return her to the field via the road.

When we arrived at the depot Sunny was standing unconcerned as a group of men formed a human fence around her. The night watchman greeted us. He had been the first to be aware of the fugitive's presence. With glee he recounted the events, "I heard something moving in the undergrowth. I thought it was probably thieves after the cars. I shouted, 'Come out!' but the rustling of the trees continued. I decided to go and have a closer look, I don't mind admitting it Missus but I thought my number was up! All I could see were two huge eyes staring straight into mine, I caught a glimpse of the dark coat and I really thought it was a lion. Before I could make a run for it, she broke cover and then I realised it was one of your cows."

I could well imagine the fright she had given the poor man, but he had found the whole event exciting. So too did the rest of the drivers, they watched in fascination as I slipped the halter over her head and

Chapter 59 – Sex in the Country

we made our way towards the road. Graham refused point blank to walk her along the road. He still hadn't forgiven her for the escapade at the show. Instead, he walked with us gesticulating wildly to car drivers to slow down as they approached us. Our lane is a very busy road early in the morning as drivers use it as a short cut to the Birmingham suburbs, this day was no exception.

We only had to walk a hundred yards to the safety of the farm. Sonny did not let me down. She strolled beside me with a nonchalant air, totally unconcerned of the traffic. Once she was safely back home I breathed a sigh of relief. I had made a decision, I could not afford to have my cows going off looking for a mate; Jock, the rapidly growing bull calf would stay as a bull and keep them happy at home.

Bert was delighted when I told him of my plans for Jock. I was still unsure but I could see the advantages of having our own bull. Graham remained totally unconvinced and said, "Mark my words it will all end in tears." I was well used to his pessimistic views and paid no heed to his comment.

Chapter 60
Dicing with Danger

Winter had now settled around the farm. The weather had not been icy but we had endured days of none stop rain. The only horses we still stabled were Fleur and Peanuts. In the winter months they were allowed out in the fields for a few hours a day. As usual I had turned them out into the field mid morning. Fleur could be a very wilful animal. She loved her food and would steal the hay from the cattle. She would flatten her ears, bare her teeth and lash out with her hooves around the hayrack. The cattle for all their size, and weaponry gave way to her, but they did not like her. So it was no surprise that when the opportunity arose they would attempt to settle some old scores with her.

The day of reckoning had arrived. At lunchtime, Gemma rushed into the house, shouting, "Ann, come quick! Fleur is lying down in the field. It looks as though she is stuck." I went immediately to see what the problem was. Sure enough, she was caught in the sheep wire fence. There was no alternative but to try and free her. We took a pair of wire cutters, and a cattle stick and proceeded to walk across the field. Our presence in the field attracted the attention of the cattle, they watched our every move. Sam was particularly interested. He was now a full grown steer; it would not be long before he was ready for slaughter. Finally, we reached Fleur. Gemma talked to her softly whilst I busied myself trying to cut through the wire.

As we were crouched on the ground we heard the unmistakable sound of heavy feet charging towards us. I looked up and fear

Chapter 60 – Dicing with Danger

gripped my body. Sam was charging towards us at full speed, he had realised that Fleur was incapacitated and he was about to get his own back. The trouble was, Gemma and I were between him and the stricken horse. We had nowhere to escape to. We were hemmed in a corner. There was no point in running, the ground was sodden and Sam could out run us easily. I stood up,. Gemma came to my side. I held out the cattle stick and like Canute trying to turn the tide I stood there helplessly as Sam continued his charge. At the last moment he saw the stick, but in the muddy field his brakes failed and he slid with considerable force on to the stick. I felt the impact ricochet up my arm. Sam stood still in his tracks, a look of confusion in his eyes, he had never been on the receiving end of the stick before. He had certainly felt it penetrate his fur and probably it bruised his skin. Whatever, mortified at the attack from his stockman, he turned away and joined the rest of the cattle. I was utterly relieved, and shocked. It was then I realised Gemma's hand was entwined with mine. In all the commotion Fleur had managed to free herself, and was uninjured. Gemma and I returned to the house for a much needed cup of tea.

As I drank my tea I asked my eighteen-year old assistant a question. "Did you realise you were holding my hand?"

Without hesitation, she replied, "I thought we were going to die out there today. I decided if that was the case we would go out together holding hands." I laughed and told her she was exaggerating the seriousness of the situation, but inwardly I knew we had experienced a close shave.

Chapter 61
Staying Put

The chilly month of November is a very important in the Cat Show Calendar; the most prestigious show of the year is held. It is given the grand title, The Supreme. It is the cat world's equivalent to Crufts. I was surprised to be asked by the Somali Cat Club to exhibit Redman; they wanted him on display for all to see. To receive the invitation was a great honour, but I had misgivings. Redman behaved impeccably most of the time, but he still had a weakness where blondes were concerned. Unlike many men, he saw red when confronted by a fair-haired person. After much deliberation I decided to take him along.

We arrived at the vast show hall and were directed to a vet. This is the usual procedure as all exhibits are examined to make sure they are completely fit. We were assigned to a blonde female vet, I approached the table and said, "I'm sorry but my cat does not belong to the school of thought that gentlemen prefer blondes. In fact he hates them. We shall have to wait and see another vet." The vet was unconcerned by my revelation. It was just another barmy cat woman in a long line that she would have to endure before the day was over. Eventually, we were vetted in by a dark haired young man; Redman was taken to his pen, and I stayed by his side for the entire show.

The public surrounded his pen. He loved the attention and glory. His behaviour was perfect. From that moment on I never saw any aggression from him again. I will never know for certain the reason he became so good-tempered, but I can surmise. When Redman joined

Chapter 61 – Staying Put

me he was only three years old, and had already experienced four homes. Everywhere he had lived previously, he had outlived his usefulness, so he had been shipped on to the next stud house. Sadly, this is a fate than can befall entire male cats. It must have come as a surprise to him, to return after a long day to the same home he had left that morning.

I made a promise to Redman that he would never leave the farm; he was home at last. I doubt he understood me, but over the many years we spent together he rewarded me with numerous show winners. Eventually he passed away through old age. I kept my word, and buried my magnificent boy under the rose bush, in sight of his stud house, where he had spent many happy hours entertaining his lady friends.

Chapter 62
A Night Vigil

Winter slowly dragged on, the heavy frosts failed to arrive but the torrential rain came with a vengeance. The fields were water logged and the stock spent most of their time housed in the buildings. Milly was due to calve in February. I hoped by then the weather would improve. Graham was due to celebrate his fortieth birthday at the end of March. My husband has always been a party animal, so I planned to give him a surprise party. The local village hall was booked, and a live band had agreed to play their repertoire of pop songs. Meg agreed to help me with the catering, invites were secretly dispatched. Slowly the plans took shape. In the meantime, the work on the farm went ahead as usual.

Milly did not disappoint me. On the due date, she went into labour. She gave birth to a bull calf in her favourite place in the field, a sheltered corner. I watched their progress intently. At first, all seemed to go well. It is normal within an hour of birth for the calf to stagger to its feet and begin to suckle. As the minutes ticked by, the new born calf did not show any interest in taking his first steps, let alone having that vital first drink which contained colostrum. Panic began to set in, I knew something was amiss. The only thing I could do was yet again call the cavalry. As always Bert arrived within minutes. With all the confidence, and experience, of a lifetime spent farming he inspected the calf. He turned to me and said, "We need to get his circulation going. Get some straw and rub his legs as hard as you can." I did as instructed, when I returned Bert was roughly slapping the calf's

Chapter 62 – A Night Vigil

chest. We spent the next ten minutes treating the animal to a bruising massage. Our efforts were rewarded as he began to stand on his own wobbly legs. Bert said, "We need to get them both in the yard, bring your car down, we will put the calf in the back. Leave the tailgate open, the old cow will then follow." Milly did just as Bert had predicted. We settled them in the yard and then Bert said, "Keep an eye on them, and make sure the calf suckles. If he hasn't drunk by six o'clock tonight, ring me." Bert left us alone with our charges. The staff and I took turns to sit in the yard and watch. They were never left alone for a moment. At the appointed time, I rang Bert and told him the calf had not suckled. Bert came straight away. We walked to the yard, Bert asked, "Are you sure he hasn't had any milk? You might have missed it."

I pointed to a deck chair in the corner, "I don't think so. One of us has sat there all the time, watching."

Bert laughed, "When I said don't take your eyes off them, I didn't realise you would take me so literally. You may not know much about farming Anna, but your stock is lucky to have you."

I was worried sick about the calf and Milly. My face portrayed my misery, and I was completely out of my depth. Bert seeing my forlorn face said, "Cheer up, Anna. We'll get them through this. Go and get a feeding bottle. I'll express some milk from the cow and we will bottle feed the wee lad."

I sighed, "Bert, you make it sound so simple. Milly is a suckler cow. In all her fifteen years she has never been milked by a human, and what if the calf won't have the bottle?"

In his familiar way Bert tipped his cap forward, scratched his head, and said, "Let's cross our bridges one at a time. Have some faith. We'll do it together."

My faith in Bert was not unfounded, the milk was expressed, and slowly the calf got to grips with the bottle. The outcome was looking more optimistic. Bert said he would return in the morning, I retired to my bed that night unaware of what was in store for me in the coming days.

As soon as I got up the next morning I went to check the calf and mother. At first nothing seemed amiss, both were lying down. As I approached, Milly made no effort to get up. If a cow is reluctant to stand a sharp slap in the middle of the back usually has the desired effect, but Milly did not respond. I had read about downer cows and I was certain this applied to Milly. I ran to the house and called Bert. Minutes later Bert strode into the yard, gave Milly a good thump on the back, and up she got. Once again my animals had made a fool of me. I was so relieved I did not notice the concern on Bert's face. He ran his expert hands over her udder and said, "You had better call the vet, she has got a touch of mastitis."

This did not worry me too much; it had happened before with one of the goats. A course of antibiotics had soon put her to rights. The vet duly arrived and administered his potions. He told me to bathe the udder three times daily and massage it well. At first Milly did not like my nursing technique and kicked at my hands and arms with a vengeance but I persevered. The day wore on, my time was spent either massaging the udder or bottle feeding the calf. Milly slowly became worse and by nightfall she was very sick indeed. She had a purulent discharge from her eyes and nose, her breathing was laboured. I decided to phone the vet once again. I told Alan her symptoms. As usual, he was very matter-of-fact. He said, "It doesn't sound good. You will have to face it, some cows die with mastitis and it looks as if this might be the scenario in this case."

I was horrified; if Milly were going to die she would not be on her own. I settled down in the yard for my vigil. Through the night her breathing became noisy, I talked to her, pleaded with her to fight the infection. I constantly wiped the discharge from her face, making her as comfortable as I could. As light dawned the crisis passed, the breathing became freer and the discharge began to abate. The staff arrived for work to find a live cow but an exhausted boss.

Over the forthcoming weeks the calf suckled from the good teats, but despite all my efforts with the infected quarter it never recovered, for the rest of her life, Milly became what is known as a three quarter cow. After his troublesome start to life, the calf thrived well. We called him Campbell. Perhaps it was because he had so much interaction with humans when he was born that he was very affectionate and followed us everywhere. Nature can be ruthless; it was exhilarating to be able to cheat death on this occasion, but you can't win all the time.

Chapter 63
Angie's Undoing

The half-term holidays were approaching. The school, which Joe and Lucy attended, had organised a three-day trip to Weston for their class. Andrew, a friend of theirs wanted to go but his parents had booked a holiday for that time. Lucy has always believed our home is open house to anyone, so true to form she said he could stay with us after they returned from the trip. The children had it all arranged; we parents could only nod our heads in agreement. The children enjoyed their field trip, and for a few days at least I would have three children to look after. Andrew had not been in the house long, when he asked me, "Do you know who has eaten my chocolate?" I was puzzled, "I'm sorry Andrew but I don't know what you are talking about."

Patiently, he explained, "My mum gave me a box of sweets and chocolate biscuits to share with Joe and Lucy whilst I was here. I left the box in the porch and someone has taken most of the things."

I was mystified, and to be honest, paid it little attention. We had plenty of goodies in the pantry, which would pacify the little boy. It was not until the next morning that I had reason to think about the mystery of the missing chocolate.

As usual, I went to let the goats out for their frolic in the Paddock. Angie lay in the stable clearly miserable and unwell. She had been fine the night before, but now she was a very sick goat. Suddenly, I remembered the box of disappearing treats, I was certain I had found my thief. Angie had always had a sweet tooth and had been known to

Life on the Funny Farm

mug customers for a mint cream. I woke Andrew and tried to ascertain how many sweets had been in the box. According to him, Angie must have munched her way through pounds of the sugary delights. There was nothing for it but to phone Alan the vet.

In due course he arrived. Blunt as ever, he said, "She has ingested too much sugar and it has poisoned her system. The problem is goats can't vomit so it will have to work through her body. It will probably do untold damage to her vital organs, and consequently she will die." Trust Alan, he always told it how it was. I began yet another vigil, but this time to no avail. My beloved Angie slipped into a coma and later that evening, passed away. She was my first goat. I loved her dearly; she gave me nine years of pleasure. I have many fond memories of her, including her collar which I have kept to this day. It does not seem right another of my goats should wear it. I also have lasting visible reminders of her life. The trees from which she destructively stripped the bark still bare the scars, the missing piece of wood from the gate which she also devoured. I suppose it should have come as no surprise to me that it would be her voracious appetite that would be the death of her.

The preparations for Graham's party were well under way, the replies to the invites were arriving in the post. Fortunately, Graham left for work long before the postman delivered the mail. Meg and I would have to cater for a hundred people to be sure there would be sufficient food. Customers were busy booking their pets in for their holidays in the summer. As usual, there was a steady supply of guests whose owners had booked an off-season break. Just before my husband's party a regular customer, Mrs. Wood had booked her pet beagle in for a two-week stay. One day, she rang in quite a state. She said, "Something dreadful has happened. Charity, my beagle got out while she was in season. I saw a black Labrador mate her and the vet has confirmed today that she is pregnant. My husband says he will divorce me if I cancel the holiday. I don't know what to do. She is due to have them while we are away. Please, can you help?"

Chapter 64
Resurrection

I saw no reason why Charity could not stay with us. She had been visiting us regularly for some years and knew me well. She could stay in the house and I would deliver her pups. I made it quite clear that whilst I would do my very best, if anything should go wrong it was at the owner's risk. Mrs. Wood agreed readily.

On the appointed day, Charity duly arrived. By looking at her I guessed the pups would not be born for at least another week, typical; just in time for the surprise party.

Other clients brought their pets to stay. Another regular was a cat called Nelson. He was a black, mean-natured cat, aptly named because he had only one eye. He was very temperamental and was not adverse to giving a well aimed strike with his claws as he was taken out of his carrier. For this reason the staff usually delegated booking him in, to yours truly. I chatted to his owner. Unlike her cat, she was a charming lady, she told me, "You are lucky to board Nelson, he's dead you know!"

I peered into the carrier. The mean green eyes stared back at me malevolently, and he was very far from dead. Curious, I asked, "What do you mean?"

She replied, "A few weeks ago, he went missing. He was gone for days. We put up notices in the area and finally a neighbour rang to say that there was a dead black cat on the verge further down the street. My husband went and found the body. It was very bedraggled and worse for wear as it had lain there sometime. We both know he was no angel but we took the body to our vet and had him cremated. A week later we got a lovely casket back with his ashes, we buried it in the garden. In all, it cost us eighty pounds but we felt we had given him a good send-off."

I continued to stare at the cat in the basket, if this wasn't Nelson, he was his double.

She continued, "It was a couple of weeks later, we were sitting watching television when we heard the cat flap rattle. My husband was annoyed that some cat was using the flap to gain entry. He went into the hall to shoo it away and seal the flap. The next thing I knew he was shouting for me, his voice sounded really strange. I went to him and there sitting bold as you like was Nelson. It gave my husband a real bad turn, you see he thought it was a ghost cat. I must admit I didn't know what to make of it until he stalked up to me; hit me across the leg in true Nelson style. I knew then he was flesh and blood."

I listened as the tale unfolded and asked, "What about the cat you had cremated?"

She answered, "Oh we never did found out who that belonged to. It's a pity that my husband never looked to see if the poor creature had two eyes. It would have saved us eighty quid."

Smiling, I said, "You ought to rename him Lazarus."

Nelson continued to visit us for many years until his owners moved from the district. Over the years his mean nature never improved, but his owners continued to love him.

Early spring saw the arrival of another of our regular guests. Bonny an exuberant Springer Spaniel was booked in for a week's holiday. She had visited us many times before and she always impressed me with her zest for life. Imagine my shock when she struggled to climb out of the car. She stood on the drive staring into space, apparently disorientated. Her back leg bore the recent scars of major surgery.

Amazed at the complete change in the dog I asked the owner, "What ever has happened to her?"

The owner replied, "She was run over, her back leg was broken, and she sustained a head injury, which has robbed her of her sight."

Chapter 64 - Resurrection

My heart went out to the young dog. I said, "She was lucky she wasn't killed, many dogs don't live to tell the tale when they argue with a car."

The owner nodded in agreement, he continued, "It was lucky the vehicle was going so slowly, but it was only to be expected."

" What do you mean?" I asked.

"Bonny must be unique. She was run over by a hearse. Our neighbour had died and we wanted to pay our respects, so we went to watch the funeral cortège. Bonny darted out straight under the wheels." He stared fondly at the dog.

I could well imagine the distress the accident had caused. I said, "I expect the people there found it hard to believe."

The owner replied, "Everyone was upset as it was, Bonny's accident just made matters worse.

On subsequent visits, it was clear that Bonny had regained the full use of her leg; it was as good as new. She managed to adapt to the loss of her sight and regained her extrovert, happy-go-lucky approach to life.

Chapter 65
Tail Ends

With the party drawing ever closer the last thing I needed was one of my animals to need my undivided attention. As always, animals choose the least convenient time to need veterinary treatment. On the Sunday a week before Graham's birthday, disaster struck. One of the colony of farm cats had gone missing some days earlier. Jim had begun life on the farm as a kitten abandoned in a cardboard box on the drive. He was not a very handsome black and white cat. He had sharp features similar to an oriental cat. What he lacked in looks he made up for in his generous nature. He was always around the farm, so when he disappeared we all feared the worst. We had scoured the hedgerows searching for him, but to no avail. It was on the Sunday he dragged himself home, he was in a very sorry state. His tail was mangled and the flesh on his back was red raw, with the smell of decaying flesh emanating from it. I rang my vet, but could get no reply. Since the departure of Angus and Shona, Neville had joined a syndicate of surgeries to cover out-of-hours emergencies. This was the first time I needed them, and the system failed. With no other option I rang another practice and explained my predicament. They agreed to treat Jim.

When I arrived at the surgery, I was met by a young woman. I was anxious about trusting a vet I did not know. I need not have worried; she was a genuine cat lover, and a gifted vet. She took one look at Jim, and knew straight away what had happened. She said, "This cat has been caught in a snare, probably one used for rabbits. He has

Chapter 65 - Tail Ends

tried to free himself by chewing through his tail. The injury is serious. I shall have to amputate the tail at the base and I'm not sure if there will be enough skin to cover the site of the operation. I can tell you now this will be a long job, with no guarantee of success. It will cost you a lot of money. If you don't want to go ahead I understand. I can put him to sleep if you wish." I replied straight away, "Go ahead and do what you can, he deserves a chance."

Jim was operated on the next day, then followed weeks of nursing. Many times we thought the flesh would never heal but gradually healthy skin began to grow again. The treatment was very painful for Jim. He never complained nor did he raise a paw in defiance. I visited the young vet regularly with Jim over a period of months. I grew to admire her. I realised that Neville could no longer provide me with the emergency service I needed, it was time for a change. What better than sign on with the practice which had done such sterling work to save Jim.

With only a few days to go before the party, Meg and I spent what little spare time we had preparing food for the buffet. Between us we prepared a feast fit for a king. Graham had no inkling of what was going on. One evening, I said, "Love, you know it's your birthday this weekend. I have booked a table at the local restaurant for Saturday night. Is that alright?"

"Sounds great to me." Replied Graham.

"There is just one other thing, the cubs have got a jumble sale early in the evening at the Village Hall and I've promised to help."

Graham sighed, "Why didn't you tell them you were going out for a meal. I suppose Joe volunteered your services."

Calmly, I said, "It won't be a problem, perhaps you can pick me up from the sale, and then we can go and eat."

Testily, he said, "I don't have a choice do I?"

I was relieved I had managed to engineer Graham's attendance at the hall, and also allow myself time to set up the last minute details. I knew when he discovered the deception he would not be annoyed.

Chapter 66
Puppies and Partying

Saturday arrived, and so did Charity's pups! From the moment I awoke it was clear that the bitch was about to whelp. Once again an animal had chosen the most inconvenient time to demand my attention. Although Charity had never given birth before, she was a natural. Throughout the morning she effortlessly gave birth to eight pups. The Labrador father had stamped his genes well and truly on them. None of them resembled a beagle in any way. The pups were large; six of them were jet black, with only a hint of white in odd little patches. The other two were a golden hue, their wrinkled faces reminded me of Winston Churchill. By lunchtime they were all suckling quite happily from their mother, who was a picture of contentment with her brood.

Now that the pups were safely into the world I could devote the afternoon to the final preparations for the party. Time flew by. I had managed to get rid of my husband for the day to one of his favourite haunts, the golf club. The food was taken to the hall, and we busied ourselves decorating the room. At five o'clock Meg and I surveyed our efforts. The hall was festooned with balloons, a huge banner proclaimed, 'Happy 40th Graham'. I returned to the farm, donned my party dress, and collected Joe and Lucy. We managed to get out of the house before Graham retuned home, he would pick us up as arranged from the jumble sale at seven thirty.

The band arrived first with all their paraphernalia. They soon set their stall out on the stage. As seven o'clock approached the guests

Chapter 66 - Puppies and Partying

began to arrive. My parents Tom and Emily were one of the first. Tom who was a keen photographer had agreed to be the official cameraman for the night. The rest of the family soon joined them. Friends came from all over the country bringing various gifts for the birthday boy.

The local contingent were last to arrive, I hardly recognised Bert and his family. They were all dressed in their Sunday best. Finally the star of the show arrived. Graham walked into the hall and was greeted by the assembled guests. It had been hard work preparing the surprise but it was all worth it when I saw the genuine delight on his face. Graham soon found me in the midst of the people. He flung his arms round me and gave me a bear hug. He urgently whispered into my ear, "There aren't any more surprises, are there? You haven't hidden a new addition have you?" "What ever do you mean?" I asked.

"Knowing you, there might be a Llama or something similar lurking in the background."

I laughed, "There is no ulterior motive, this party is just for you because I love you. But thinking about it Llamas are becoming very popular!"

The party soon got into full swing, the band played all evening. Lucy, as usual danced the night away. Graham chatted to all his friends. All too soon the evening was over. Friends who had travelled long distances returned to the farm with us and made a weekend of their visit. As I lay in bed that night I was happy in the knowledge Graham had enjoyed his surprise present. It was a week later Tom brought the photographs. He had placed them neatly in an album. It was a pleasant Spring day. Graham and I sat under the willow tree in the garden studying the photographs. The hens, ducks and geese were walking around the lawn. Anthony was displaying his beautiful plumage to his bride Cleopatra. The winter months were once more behind us. As I sat companionably with my husband, I reflected on ten years of marriage. My life had changed so much. I had done things since my marriage that I had never even dreamed of. One thing was certain I could not have been more content in my little piece of England.

We reached the end of the photograph album. It would serve as a reminder of the party for the rest of our lives. As Graham went to close the book, he caught sight of the last page. Instead of a photo-

Life on the Funny Farm

graph, Tom had written the following. 'Today is the first day of the rest of your life.' I could not help but wonder what adventures the next ten years would bring!